Socialism in the 21st century
the way forward for anti-capitalism

by Hannah Sell

Socialism in the 21st century -
the way forward for anti-capitalism
by Hannah Sell
© Socialist Publications 2002

First Edition August 2002
Scond Edition February 2006
Classification: Hannah Sell
Socialism in the 21st century - the way forward for anti-capitalism
Politics/Economics

ISBN 1-870958 23 3 pbk

A catalogue record for this book is available
from the British Library

Published by Socialist Publications (formerly Fortress Books)
for The Socialist Party

Typeset by Kavita Graphics
dennis@kavitagraphics.co.uk
Typeset in Usherwood 9 pt
Printed by Russell Press (Nottingham)

Distribution by Socialist Books
PO Box 24697, London, E11 1YD
Telephone +44 (0)20 8988 8777

socialism 21st century ◎

Acknowledgements

I would like to thank all the many people who suggested additions and gave constructive criticism. Particular thanks are due to Manny Thain for his helpful suggestions and meticulous proof reading and to Dennis Rudd for layout and design.

About the Author

Hannah Sell is the Campaigns Organiser for the Socialist Party. She has been active in socialist politics from an early age, becoming a supporter of the Militant Tendency at 14 years of age having played a leading role in school student strikes in Wolverhampton. In 1988, when she was 17, Hannah was elected to the Labour Party's National Executive Committee representing the Labour Party Young Socialists (LPYS). She was the last LPYS representative on the NEC. The right-wing leadership of the Labour Party, desperate to drive socialist policies out of the party, closed the LPYS down in 1989.

Hannah went on to be National Secretary of Youth Against Racism in Europe (YRE) from 1992-95. YRE played a leading role in the battle against the neo-Nazi British National Party (BNP) in the early 1990s - co-organising the 50,000 strong march on the BNP's HQ in Welling, London. Hannah has been a member of the Socialist Party since it was founded in 1993 (then called Militant Labour) and sits on its Executive Committee.

Introduction to the 2006 edition

Just six months after the first edition of Socialism in the 21st century was published two million people took to the streets of Britain on 15 February 2003 to oppose the impending war on Iraq. It was probably the biggest single demonstration in Britain's history and it formed part of what was certainly the biggest ever simultaneous global movement.

This magnificent movement shook governments to their foundations and graphically showed the internationalism and willingness to struggle of millions of ordinary people; yet it did not prevent the war in Iraq.

In the minds of millions this raised the question: are we – the working class, the poor, the oppressed – powerless to change things in the face of massive, seemingly all-powerful, corporations and the governments that do their bidding?

The answer is an unequivocal no. The world's poor and oppressed have enormous power if we unite together and rise from our knees. While it would have taken more action to stop the war machine, particularly mass workplace stoppages – the potential for which was glimpsed in the heroic school student strikes that took place – the anti-war movement nonetheless terrified the ruling classes worldwide. In Britain Blair clung to power by a thread. It was not for nothing that the New York Times declared on 17 February 2003 that there were now, "two superpowers on the planet: the United States and world public opinion." [1]

And while the Iraq war can be said to have strengthened a potential superpower – mass action - it also enormously weakened and undermined the other superpower – US imperialism. George Bush and his entourage imagined that invading Iraq would strengthen the power and prestige of US imperialism. Instead it has revealed all of its weaknesses on the international stage and increasingly at home. Around 60% of the US population now say that the war was wrong and only 40% support George Bush.

It is not only against the war that the 'new superpower' has flexed its muscles. Struggle on other issues has also increased. More and more people are fighting back -from the Nigerian workers who over the last five years have taken part in seven general strikes and mass protests against fuel price hikes, to the Bolivian working class and oppressed struggling for nationalisation of their oil and gas industries, to the New York transport workers, and the French and Dutch workers who defied their governments to vote 'no' to continued privatisation and cuts in the referendums on the European constitution.

And when we rise from our knees we can win victories. In Britain, the mere threat of 1.5 million workers taking strike action forced the government to partially retreat over plans to increase the retirement age for public sector workers. There are other examples of workers in Britain – like the nursery nurses in Scotland and the bus drivers in Stoke – who have been able to win victories as a result of strike action. In Ireland, with assistance of the Socialist Party, Turkish immigrant workers – employed by the construction company Gama

– who had had the bulk of their wages illegally withheld, were recently able to win thousands of euros in back pay, at the same time as revealing to the world a cesspit of similar scandals. In the aftermath of the Gama strike the Irish Ferries dispute erupted, with 100,000 workers taking part in demonstrations during a national half-day strike demanding decent pay for immigrant workers on Irish Ferries.

Worldwide there are a very many more examples of the oppressed defeating their oppressors. But there are not enough. The most common story is still of the privateers, asset strippers and thieves getting away with riding roughshod over the rest of humanity. And even when we do win victories they are never permanent. Capitalism's remorseless drive to maximise profits equals a relentless 'race to the bottom' in terms of working-class peoples conditions of life and work, which can only be resisted by determined struggle.

If further evidence were needed that capitalism is incapable of taking society forward; the last four years have provided it. Not only the ongoing nightmare of the occupation of Iraq – which has led to the death of many tens of thousands of Iraqis and over 2,000 'coalition' soldiers – but also the inability of capitalism to take any effective action to prevent the decimation of our environment. In some ways, the most graphic illustration of capitalism's crisis is its inability to cope with natural disasters - whether the tsunami at the end of 2004, or the South Asian earthquake or Hurricane Katrina last year. The countless thousands who died unnecessarily, and those still homeless -including in the US, the richest nation on the planet - stand as a complete condemnation of the profit system.

By contrast, the preparedness of ordinary people worldwide to give to assist the victims of disaster, repeatedly putting the puny efforts of governments to shame, stand as a testament to the strength of human solidarity.

It is therefore no surprise that the years since the first edition of Socialism in the 21st Century was written have seen an increased interest in anti-capitalist ideas in general, and specifically in a socialist alternative. The anti-war movement, in particular, radicalised a generation, and has led some of them to actively seek out socialist ideas.

At this stage, it is still a minority who have become conscious socialists, but it is a growing minority. Socialism in the 21st Century was written with the aim of assisting workers and young people who were interested in socialist ideas to find out more. There is no doubt that this second edition has a potentially broader audience than the first.

Today, in Britain, around 150 companies completely dominate the lives of 60 million people. Worldwide, the richest 356 people enjoy a combined wealth that is greater than the annual income of 40% of the human race. This book gives an outline of how a democratically planned socialist economy could harness the vast wealth of capitalism to meet the needs of humanity instead of lining the pockets of a few. At the same time, it raises some of the most important tasks that face socialists in this period – such as the need to lead struggles to defend workers' living conditions against the rapacious greed of the multinationals and the need to build new mass workers' parties which represent the interests of working-class people. It links these tasks to the struggle for 'socialism in the 21st century'.

Hannah Sell - January 2006

Note: 1 New York Times, February 17, 2003

Introduction
to first edition

This book argues the case for socialism. Why are you and other readers interested in such a book? Why are growing numbers of people considering becoming socialists? It is clearly not because socialism is widely publicised. None of the major political parties are socialist, socialism does not feature on the national curriculum in schools, and the TV is not packed with programmes arguing in favour of it. On the contrary, if you were to judge purely by the media, parliament, or the education system, you would decide that socialism is a spent force

And yet, it clearly isn't. Ideas traditionally associated with the left are increasingly popular. In a Mori poll in 2001, for example, 72% of people supported the re-nationalisation of the railway system, despite none of the major political parties arguing for it. Growing numbers of young people are taking part in anti-capitalist demonstrations. In the last year significant swings to the left have taken place in several trade unions with self-professed socialists being elected as national leaders. And more people are taking strike action - such as local government and railway workers.

None of this has been caused by 'socialist propaganda'. On the contrary, most people who support re-nationalisation, who have been on anti-capitalist demonstrations, on strike, or have voted for a left-wing trade union leader would not call themselves socialists. But an arrow tracing their political trajectory would point clearly towards the left. Broadly speaking they are moving in a socialist direction. The reason for this is fundamentally simple: many people do not like the way the world is at the moment.

No wonder. In Britain today almost 14 million men, women and children live below the poverty line. Over the last decade inequality has risen faster in Britain than in any other country in the world apart from New Zealand. Yet for a few, Britain is truly booming and we have the biggest gap between rich and poor since records began.

Internationally, 815 million people worldwide go hungry. We live on a planet where 55% of the 12 million child deaths each year are caused by malnutrition. And it's getting worse. According to the United Nations, the poorest countries are worse off now than they were 30 years ago. On the basis of current trends, the numbers living in absolute poverty - that is, on less than a dollar a day - will increase by ten million a year for the next 15 years. The Aids epidemic has already killed 25 million people and is predicted to kill a further 68 million in the coming decades. In Botswana alone, 39% of the adult population have HIV/Aids.

Meanwhile in the US, the richest country on earth, the wealthiest 1% has seen their incomes increase by 157% in real terms since 1979. By contrast, the bottom 20% are actually making $100 less a year in real terms, 45 million people live below the poverty line and over 40% have no medical cover. Despite all the advanced technology and wealth available to the US, more than 32 million people have a life expectancy of less than 60 years.

4 SOCIALISM IN THE 21ST CENTURY

It is not mainly the arguments of socialists that are changing peoples' outlook, it is their experience of the system we live under - capitalism. Ten years ago capitalism declared victory when the Soviet Union collapsed. What existed in the Soviet Union and Eastern Europe was not genuine socialism but a grotesque caricature of it. Nonetheless, its failure was a golden opportunity for capitalism worldwide.

American philosopher Francis Fukuyama put it bluntly in 1989: "What we are witnessing is not just the end of the Cold War [the post-1945 conflict between US imperialism and the Soviet Union] but the end of history as such: that is, the end point of man's ideological evolution and the universalism of Western liberal democracy."

Ten years after this declaration of the "end point of man's ideological development", and even Fukuyama has changed his tune. The cold war is supposed to be over but arms spending totalled $804 billion in 2000, an average of $130 a person. Humanity's supposedly wondrous endpoint is a world of war, poverty, dictatorship and, above all, incredible inequality.

Millions of people are fighting back against the reality of Fukuyama's nirvana. They are the Bolivian masses who rose up and prevented the privatisation of their water supply and the Argentinians who overthrew four presidents in two weeks. They are the ten million Indian workers who took strike action against privatisation. They are the workers in Spain who held a one-day general strike against attacks unemployment rights, and the workers in Italy who have mobilised in their millions against the right-wing government of Silvio Berlusconi. At the same time as the poor and oppressed of entire countries are fighting back against the effects of capitalism, a minority are beginning to consciously look for an alternative system. If you look up 'capitalism' in the Collins English Dictionary it suggests you compare it with the alternative - 'socialism'. Socialist ideas have been developed over centuries in the course of humanity's fight for a better life. Today they remain the only viable alternative in an increasingly unstable and brutal, capitalist world. It is this reality that ensures that socialism is not a spent force but the wave of the future.

Hannah Sell - August 2002

Britain at the start of the 21st century

Over the last decade our city centres have been transformed. There are shiny new shopping malls and fancy shops that used to be found only in London. Coffee bars and bistros abound. Cinema multiplexes offer all the latest blockbusters five or ten times daily. In the big cities, supermarkets are open 24-hours a day for the consumers' convenience. In our homes and about our persons many of us possess electronic hardware that we could scarcely have imagined ten or 15 years ago.

But the gleaming towers of commerce and the products that they sell are only one side of the picture. Britain has been transformed in other, more fundamental, ways. Outside the upgraded city centres, in the housing estates and suburbs where people live, conditions have also changed – not for the better but for the worse.

The Victorians used to say that it is not work but worry that kills. The deterioration in the quality of life for millions in Britain can be summed up as an increase in

from 'dark satanic mills' to dark satanic ruins?

worry – in the stresses and strains of daily life. For those in work, hours have got longer and work has got harder. Secure jobs are increasingly rare. Millions feel that they are clinging by the fingertips to the cliff face of a 'civilised' existence – just one pay cheque away from the abyss of grinding poverty. For those out of work, making ends meet is a constant struggle, sometimes in vain. Housing and childcare are horrendously expensive. Transport is expensive and chaotic. The NHS seems to be on the brink of collapse. Violent crime, particularly by and against young people, is on the increase.

The neo-liberal policies (attacks on workers' rights, working and living conditions, the privatisation of industry and social services, etc) most associated with this increase in poverty and misery were known as Thatcherism. Margaret Thatcher became Tory prime minister in 1979. Ironically, the previous Labour government had started implementing the policies which she then carried out on a grand scale. By 1987 Thatcher had cut £12 billion from the welfare state. As a result, basic state benefits for the unemployed covered only 55% of the basic necessities of life. The number of working poor had increased by 300%. By the time she was forced out of power, her 'home-owning democracy' had led to a 300% increase in private-sector rents and a 100% increase in the rents of the dwindling number of council houses.

The money that Thatcher saved was poured into the pockets of the very rich. One tax cut alone gave the richest 550,000 people an extra £33,000 a year each. Altogether, billions were transferred from the pockets of the majority into the moneybags of the very rich.

Thatcher famously said that there is 'no such thing as society', only individuals and families. It wasn't and isn't true. But her government's policies ripped huge chunks out of the basic support system that the welfare state provided for working-class people and in doing so undermined the fabric of society. A state pension which provided the bare minimums of life in old age, council housing for those who could not afford (or did not want) to buy, and the right of 16- and 17-year-olds to claim benefits, all this and more was taken away. Millions have been left with only the flimsiest of safety nets. The inevitable result is a huge increase in poverty and all that brings with it.

The results for the poorest are graphic and brutal. The death rate among those below the poverty line is four times that of the most affluent. For homeless people living on the street the average life expectancy is 47 years – as low as the very poorest countries on the planet. Over the last 20 years the suicide rate for young men has increased by 45%.

Nor were Thatcher's policies limited to trying to remove the safety net. The Tories also destroyed whole sections of heavy industry that had provided relatively well-paid jobs. When Thatcher became prime minister, Britain - the first major capitalist power on the planet - had been in inglorious decline for a century and the process was accelerating. Thatcher and her cronies decided to try and resuscitate British capitalism by turning away from manufacturing and towards the service sector. In doing so she also wanted to try and break the power of the trade unions. Twenty years on and manufacturing industry has been devastated. Manufacturing jobs have been replaced by 'McJobs'. Call centres have replaced factories. Low-paid, insecure work has become the norm.

Thatcherism continued...

Thatcher was no aberration. The neo-liberal policies that she pioneered stemmed from capitalism's economic crisis and were adopted worldwide. Thatcher herself met her comeuppance in 1991. A mass movement against the poll tax, 18 million strong, led to the overthrow of the 'Iron Lady'. But while Thatcher and her hated tax have gone, her policies continue unabated.

The election of New Labour in 1997 represented an overwhelming and ferocious desire of the majority of the people for change. At the same time, the low turnout reflected a justified feeling from many that New Labour would not deliver such change.

New Labour has pursued a continuation of Tory policies. Blairism is, in essence, Thatcherism delivered with added smarm. As a result, an extra 400,000 pensioners are living in poverty since 1997. In Labour's first two years in office a further 100,000 children fell below the poverty line. Just like the Tories, New Labour sees the untrammelled market economy (that is, capitalism at its most naked) as the only way of running Britain. The twice-disgraced ex-minister and architect of Blairism, Peter Mandelson, summed up the approach in typically brazen fashion when he declared that New Labour aims to establish "the most business friendly environment in the world".[1]

After 18 years of Tory rule it seemed that there were no public services left to privatise. But New Labour wants to privatise anything that remains, including the maintenance of nuclear weapons and London Underground, which even most of big business is opposed to privatising. The government is selling off ever more public housing, resulting in huge rent rises. In 1999, 71,265 people were evicted through the courts from rented accommodation. This is the highest rate for over 20 years. Any remaining social housing is being brought 'in line' with market rents. There has been a staggering 365% increase in evictions from social housing since New Labour came to power!

In the health service more and more services are being handed over to private contractors. The same is true in education and local government. Without exception this means worse wages and conditions for the staff and worse services for the public. Despite New Labour's determination to ignore the facts, it is blindingly obvious that private companies only run public services for one reason: to make profits. In the first six months of 2000 the pre-tax profits of Laing, the building firm, rose by 70%. The increase was largely due to its involvement in Private Finance Initiatives (PFI – the government's favourite privatisation scheme). Serco, the facilities and contracting managing group, saw a 13% rise in its profits in the first six months of 2000. It openly explains that this is due to "the increasing shift by government to use private funding for public infrastructure".[2] What this means is that ever increasing amounts of taxpayers' money are going into the bank accounts of private companies instead of into public services.

The resulting services are generally expensive and substandard. The first NHS hospital to be built under PFI opened in Carlisle in June 2000. In the first three months, shoddy, cheapskate building led to a series of disasters. These included two ceilings collapsing because of cheap, plastic piping joints, an inadequate sewerage system leading to filth flooding the operating theatre, and expensive trolleys having to be made specially because the standard ones did not fit. The transparent roof results in temperatures in excess of 33C on sunny days as there is no air-conditioning.

And as the stock markets tumble and the British economy slides into recession many of the companies involved in PFI will find their profits under threat. Unless it is prepared to bring privatised services back into public ownership, New Labour will end up pouring public funds into subsidising big-business efforts to leech the public sector dry. This is what happened with Railtrack before New Labour was eventually and reluctantly forced to partially renationalise it.

It is true that in his last spending review, finance minister Gordon Brown promised increased funding for education and health, although the figures do not compensate for the previous five years of continual underinvestment. Even if all the money is forthcoming, however, public spending will still be lower than it was in 14 of the 18 years of Tory government. And Brown's funding pledge is combined with a further onslaught on the rights and conditions of public-sector workers and even more privatisation. Once again, a large percentage of the money will end up in the pockets of major company executives.

Big-business Britain

Journalist and environmental campaigner, George Monbiot, described how New Labour's pet project, the Dome, encapsulated its attitude to the big companies: "The Millennium Dome exhibits the work of some of our most cherished national institutions: the American companies Manpower, Ford and McDonald's. Its Body Zone was sponsored by the chemist chain Boots, its Mind Zone by the weapons manufacturer British Aerospace and the Learning Zone by the supermarket Tesco. The 'Our Town' stage, where 'the diversity of local culture is celebrated' was financed by that guardian of cultural diversity, McDonald's."[3]

What was true of the Dome is also true, on a far grander scale, for the whole of British society. For example, it has always been the case that capitalism means there is one law for the rich and another for the poor. Since New Labour came to power, however, the police have more reason than ever to go easy on big-business crime: "The saddles used by the City of London's mounted police now bear the logo of HSBC, after the bank helped to save the division from closure by meeting some of its costs. Crime prevention in Cleveland is sponsored by General Accident Insurance and a company called Modern Security. In Avon and Somerset law and order was, until recently, underwritten by the drinks chain Threshers!"[4]

Drowning in riches

For those at the very top of society New Labour has certainly delivered. After 18 years of the Tories giving money to the rich, one of the first acts of the current government was to cut corporation tax again. In 2000 the highest paid directors of the FTSE-100 companies (the top 100 on the stock exchange) earned 48 times the pay of the average employee. At the end of 2001, four directors received bonuses worth a total of £43 million.

The argument of the market is that good bosses are worth what they receive. Why an 'efficient' business person is worth so much more than a doctor, nurse or firefighter is never explained. In any case, in Britain today every kind of boss gets showered in riches. In fact, there is now a kind of bonus for incompetent bosses, a 'golden parachute', where a huge bonus is paid for those incapable of doing their jobs. Recently, the top man at NatWest was given £3 million to sweeten his sacking while the chief executive of Sainsbury's received £1.2 million to clear his desk sharpish. Compare this to what happens to the rest of us when we lose our jobs. Take the example of WorldCom. The former boss of WorldCom, the company responsible for the biggest corporate fraud in history, is getting a pension pay-off of $1.5 million a year (£1m). Meanwhile, 20% of the 17,000 WorldCom workers who have lost their jobs as a result of the fraud have not received a cent.

No party for the working class

New Labour has gone over to support for the free market, lock, stock and barrel. It is, in that sense, no different to the other major parties. Prime minister Tony Blair tells us that he is proud to receive big-business donations even though – from Bernie Ecclestone, the Formula One racing millionaire onwards – working people are disgusted by sleazy big-business influence over New Labour. One-third of Labour Party funds now comes from corporate donors. For the first time ever this is more than the income from trade unions. At New Labour's 2000 conference fewer than 2,000 of the 20,000 who attended were party delegates. The rest were corporate sponsors, lobbyists and journalists. There were a record 188 corporate exhibitors who paid about £900,000 for the privilege of displaying their wares.

The concept behind the foundation of the Labour Party - that working people should have independent political representation - has been utterly jettisoned by New Labour. Instead, Blair promotes a class 'partnership' where we all work together for the 'common good'. But what is the common good? The interests of working-class and middle-class people, and the interests of the owners of the big corporations are poles apart. To combine them is like trying to mix oil and water. When the government introduces private finance into a hospital no amount of spin will make the interests of the hospital workers, patients and the local community the same as the interests of the private company taking the contract. The former are interested primarily in running an effective hospital that looks after people and saves lives; the latter is interested in making a profit! These two interests are not complimentary, they are diametrically opposed. The reality of Blair & Co's policies – graphically proven by 18 long, hard years under the Tories – is that the majority of the population is losing out to the big businessmen and women.

Blair has openly admitted that he sees New Labour as a version of the US Democrats – that is, as a party of big business. In the US magazine, Talk, he stated: "It has been taboo in the Labour Party even to talk about the American Democrats. You could talk about the Swedish social democrats or the French socialists, but this was taboo. It struck me when I was reading the speeches of people like Bill Clinton that what they were saying was precisely what I felt the Labour Party should be about."

In the same article Blair even regrets that workers ever formed their own independent party by splitting from the Liberals and founding the Labour Party a century ago: "When it was formed, out of its dissent from the Liberal Party... the Labour Party suffered as a result. It was more narrow in its base, it was more doctrinaire in its views, and it lost an essential Liberal strand of radical thought. And the truth of the matter is that people like myself in the Labour Party today and people like Charles Kennedy and the Liberal Democrats, we basically are driven by the same value systems."

Blair has succeeded in his mission: he has deprived the working people in Britain of any kind of political representation. Instead, we have New Labour, a party that claims the impossible: that it represents the billionaires and the working people at the same time. The result is a party that, on every occasion without exception, backs the millionaires against the millions of working-class people who voted it into power.

Could things be different?

I n the Houses of Parliament serious debate is a distant memory. On every crucial issue the three main parties are in almost complete agreement. With a few exceptions MPs accept the policies of neo-liberalism as an article of faith. Their belief in the necessity of privatisation and cuts to the public sector show just how far they are removed from the lives of ordinary people, who are overwhelmingly in favour of a turn away from the policies of the last 20 years. But the lack of a mass socialist alternative to the endless stream of sameness that pours from parliament, leaves millions knowing what they are against but as yet unsure of whether an alternative is possible.

In an article in The Guardian entitled Coalition of Dreamers, journalist Polly Toynbee ridiculed the socialist challenge for the 2001 general election. Describing Socialist Party councillor Dave Nellist as a "sincere and decent man - but more vicar than politician", she commented on the programme he had put forward: "Their policies? Take a blank piece of paper, think blue sky and green fields and dream of

labour's landslide - cartoon: alan hardman

a world that is a better place than this, unfallen angels in an Eden of goodness where all manner of things shall be well. Every adult and child will be lifted out of poverty, benefits will be restored to 16-year-olds, pensioners will not be means tested so all get the minimum income guarantee, rail and buses renationalised... and a whole lot more besides."

Toynbee, as a right-wing Labour Party member, unsurprisingly writes off socialist policies as utopian. But why can't these modest demands be achieved? Modern capitalism has created riches beyond the wildest dreams of our grandparents and great-grandparents, with the potential for far more. Yet we are constantly being told that we have no choice but to accept the erosion of our quality of life, increased poverty, worsening public services and longer working hours.

But why? Humankind has developed science and technique to a level that was unimaginable to previous generations. While still very limited, our understanding of everything from the stars above us to the secrets of our own bodies and minds is unparalleled. Humanity is capable of space exploration, has mapped the human genome, can modify genes and clone animals, yet we cannot feed the world on the basis of capitalism. For most of human history it has not been possible to satisfy even the most basic human needs. Now, as a result of the labour and ingenuity of working people, the potential exists to eliminate want forever. The barrier to achieving this is the capitalist system itself. Based as it is on the private ownership of the productive forces (factories, offices, science and technique), capitalism creates immense inequality and deprivation when the potential exists for providing the material components of a decent life for all.

There is no lack of wealth in Britain. In one year, from 1996-97, Britain's richest 500 people increased their wealth by £16.3 billion. That means that when New Labour was swept to power the collective fortune of those 500 added up to about £87 billion. That was £14 billion more than the combined annual expenditure on child benefit for seven million children, disability payments for 6.5 million people, and eleven million pensions. The reason that the lives of working people have continued to worsen under Blair is simple - New Labour accepts every dictat of the 'free market' with just as much enthusiasm as the Tories did before. From birth to death our lives are hampered and distorted by the capitalists' drive for profit.

Childcare

There are 6,000 nurseries in Britain. Only 240 of them are run on a 'not for profit' basis. On average the cost of pre-school childcare for two children is £6,000 per year, more than the average family spends on housing. Childcare in Britain is the least regulated, hardest to obtain and most expensive of any country in the European Union. Lack of decent childcare means that increasing numbers of parents, in particular women, do not have the choice of going out to work. Others are forced to rely on unqualified child carers. New Labour's solution has been to introduce the Working Families Tax Credit (WFTC) and some parents are able to struggle through with this. In total, the government spends around £5 million a year on helping pay for childcare via the WFTC. This provides a minimal level of help but much more is needed. New Labour has recently promised more money for nurseries, but these will not be publicly owned. Instead of handing money over to private nurseries, it would make far more sense to spend the money building and directly funding free, publicly-owned nurseries, after-school and holiday clubs, with fully qualified, decently paid staff.

Schools

After five years of underinvestment New Labour is now promising £7 billion extra for schools. This is welcome but it will not solve the problems. Spending on education will still fall below the 7% of national income that even Mandelson has admitted is really needed. And the £7 billion will not be used to improve the general standard of education. On the contrary, it is being linked to the complete destruction of comprehensive education and the wholesale reintroduction of selective schools. Comprehensive education, based on the development of all-round skills, was an attempt to partially overcome the greed and anarchy of the market which, of course, favours the children of the rich. Despite the limitations of the comprehensive system, its abolition will be a severe step backwards.

New Labour is replacing what remains of it with a system where 'successful' schools will be rewarded with more money. Meanwhile, the schools at the bottom of the league tables, in the areas of greatest poverty, will get no extra funds and could even be threatened with closure. New Labour is inviting big-business companies, like McDonald's, Shell and Schweppes, to make profits from our schools. If New Labour's plans are fully realised, tens of thousands of working-class young people will be condemned to second-class sink schools that 'teach' students how to work in burger bars or petrol stations.

The £7 billion New Labour has promised could be used differently. It would be enough to pay for the training of the 27,000 extra teachers needed just to return class sizes to the level they were at ten years ago. Instead, New Labour is concentrating on increasing the numbers of very low-paid, unqualified classroom assistants who are being expected to do the work of qualified teachers. The government is actively discouraging people from entering teaching. New Labour's education minister, Estelle Morris, even declared that teachers are "potty" for wanting to work a 35-hour week – hardly an incentive for going on a teacher training course!

Higher education

New Labour came to power proclaiming that its priority was "education, education, education". It then abolished all student grants and introduced tuition fees. Now one in six students drop out of college as a result of poverty. Increasingly, the children of working-class families simply cannot afford a university education. Those who struggle through have to work long hours to fund their studies and still end up with the millstone of thousands of pounds worth of debt around their necks.

Total applications for university fell by 2% in 1999/2000, with the reductions coming overwhelmingly from the poorest sections of society. Mature students have also been hard hit. In the same period, applications from men over 25 years old fell by 6.5%.

The introduction of fees is the top of a slippery slope. The Russell Group, made up of the vice-chancellors of the 19 'most prestigious' universities, wants to add its own 'top-up' fees to the current tuition fees. If they get their way, universities like Oxford and Cambridge will charge £16,000 a year – moving towards the levels of fees charged by their US equivalents, Harvard and Yale.

Education should be a right for all, not just for a privileged few. Under capitalism this has never truly been the case, but reforms that were won in the past – such as the student grant – vastly improved the opportunities of working-class students. We are now moving back towards the days when 'high quality' education was only for the elite.

The cost of abolishing tuition fees, reintroducing a full grant for all students comparable to its 1979 level (around £4,200, before 21 years of cuts began), along with the reintroduction of the right to claim benefits outside of term-time, would be about £3 billion a year. To put the figure of £3 billion into context it is equal to the profits of BP for the last six months of 2000 alone!

Housing

In 2000 there were over 410,000 people recognised as homeless in England.[5] Millions of people are forced to live in substandard, overcrowded, private rented housing – a return to the extreme exploitation and extortion of the Rachmanite landlords of the 1950s-60s. Council housing, which was built to provide an alternative to the hovels of Rachman and his ilk, is being systematically privatised. Once transferred out of council control, tenants lose their secured tenancy agreements for less protected, 'assured' tenancies. On average, rents immediately go up by £10 a week.

There is a desperate need for a large increase in the amount of affordable, pleasant and good quality social housing. Yet New Labour has not reversed Tory policy. Instead, it has stepped up the council house sell-offs. Government spending on housing has fallen dramatically. In 1998 prices, the government in the 1970s spent an average of £10.2 billion a year on housing. In the 1990s that had fallen to £7.2 billion. From 1999 to 2001 only 400 council houses were built in the whole of Britain! This compares to 28,000 other types of 'social' housing, almost always run by commercially orientated housing associations where rents are more expensive.

What social housing does exist is increasingly expensive. While Prince Michael of Kent has been able to find a bargain five-bedroom home in Kensington Palace for a mere £69 a week, the rest of us would have difficulty finding a bed-sit for that amount. In the last ten years council and other social landlords' rents have virtually doubled, while private-sector rents have increased by 90%.[6]

Lord Best, director of the Joseph Rowntree Foundation, summed up the situation: "House building is the worst since the early 1920s. The key to easing homelessness is actually simple. Build more affordable homes."[7]

Merely lifting the 'ring-fencing' restrictions – the Tory policy which prevented local authorities from spending the money from council house sales on social housing – would provide an extra £6.5 billion. Even using the 25% that New Labour has legally released from ring-fencing would be enough to provide at least 100,000 new or refurbished homes, although that would only be a fraction of what is needed and possible. After all, from 1949–54 an average of 230,000 council houses were built each year.[8]

A repetition of this would be a significant step towards solving today's housing crisis. And as a by-product, housing benefit costs would be slashed. In the last ten years housing benefit payments have doubled to £11.2 billion per year. Most of this money is stuffed straight into the pockets of private landlords in return for expensive and often substandard accommodation.

Of course, a socialist government would have to take the protection of the environment into account when building housing. At the moment the big construction companies build purely for profit with little concern for the environment, the standard or affordability of the housing. A mass house-building programme would mean careful planning to ensure the protection of green spaces. In many cases, it would be possible to build on fully decontaminated brownfield sites (abandoned land formerly used for industrial purposes). Moreover, pleasant and safe homes for all forms part of a decent environment.

Manufacturing jobs

As factories and steel plants have closed or had their workforces cut to the bone, all the government has done is to stand aside and wring its hands. In the past, even Tory governments intervened in the economy occasionally. Tory prime minister, Ted Heath, for example, nationalised Rolls Royce in the early 1970s. Clearly, the Tories were acting in the interests of big business, propping up industries before selling them back to the fat cats at rock bottom prices. New Labour, however, is so opposed to public ownership that it is unwilling even to do that. The failure of Railtrack, as a result of its catastrophic mismanagement of the rail system, forced the government to step in and reluctantly partially renationalise the railways, yet it is continuing with plans to privatise London Underground. In order to get big business to invest, a guaranteed annual profit of 15% is being promised, even if the service deteriorates. New Labour is totally opposed to any government intervention in industry. This means it is prepared to stand and fiddle while the remnants of British manufacturing burns.

Hundreds of millions of pounds of public money are being spent picking up the pieces in Dagenham, Birmingham, Wales and all the other places where factories have closed or jobs have been slashed. The cost comes from the loss of tax and National Insurance income, the increase in benefit claimants, and the unquantifiable social costs such as the extra strain on the health and welfare system. Rather than spend that money dealing with the aftermath of cuts and closure, it would be far better to invest it in keeping the industry concerned alive and, if necessary, developing new, more socially-useful production. For example, there is no need for all car plants to continue with their current production. Workers should be asked what the best use of their skills would be. Options might include environmentally friendly cars, buses or trams. In the mid-1970s, workers at Lucas Aerospace, the weapons manufacturer, produced an alternative plan of production. They worked out that their production lines could easily be altered to produce kidney machines, electronic wheelchairs and a number of other products far more useful to humanity than weaponry.

But such huge public investment should not be yet another subsidy to private companies' profits. Government intervention and public investment should be matched by public ownership and control. It would then be possible for workers in individual plants, together with representatives of workers throughout industry, could draw up a new plan of production to better meet the transport needs of the whole of society.

Pensions

New Labour insulted pensioners in 1999 with a pathetic 75p increase in the pension. Since then the government has adamantly refused to restore the link between pensions and earnings. Pensioners should receive an immediate 50% increase, and this should be extended to all state benefits. The link between pensions and earnings should be restored. These measures would cost around £15 billion a year. In addition, pensioners, having contributed to society all their lives, should be entitled to free housing, heating, telephone and travel. This could be easily paid for. There is currently an £8 billion surplus in the National Insurance fund. Reversing the changes made by the Tories to the National Insurance paid by companies would raise another £5 billion a year. This, together with reallocating New Labour's proposed £3.5 billion increase in defence spending, would raise enough money.

A constant battle

These examples prove the lie in 'Prudence' Brown's messianic belief that New Labour has no choice but to prostrate itself before the 'free market', and therefore accept the increasing gap between the rich and the poor. This is demonstrated in the starkest terms in a report by the Joseph Rowntree Foundation which calculated the effects of a modest redistribution of wealth and income which could return the situation to where it was in 1983. That was four years into Thatcher's reign, hardly an egalitarian society. Nonetheless, it would prevent about 7,500 deaths a year among the under-65s. In addition, the report stated that ending long-term unemployment would prevent another 2,500 premature deaths annually, and that achieving the government's supposed target of eliminating child poverty within a generation would save the lives of 1,400 children under the age of 15 every year.

Such modest improvements could be achieved relatively simply but capitalism is incapable of implementing them fully or lastingly. Under this system we have to battle constantly for every single improvement in our lives. Capitalism means that as soon as we let our guard down the bosses try and take every concession back. Because capitalism is based on the drive for profit – and profit is, in reality, the unpaid labour of the working class – every improvement in our living standards, every wage increase and improvement in the welfare state results in lower profits for the capitalists. That is why the ruling class would have us believe that it is utopian romanticism to dare to imagine that we can achieve even the basic proposals of the Rowntree Foundation. Real equality will only ever be achieved on the basis of abolishing capitalism. Until we succeed in doing that we will face a ceaseless and unrelenting struggle to defend our standards of living.

Alice in Wonderland

From a 'rational' point of view capitalism is a crazy way of running the world. Even though unemployment is relatively low at the moment in Britain (although this will change as recession hits the economy), there are still vast tracts of mass unemployment. The reality is far bleaker than the official figures suggest. In the North of England, Wales and Scotland, the destruction of manufacturing means that jobs are hard to come by. Even in the South, in the inner cities up to a third of young black people are unemployed. The real number of people looking for work or on government training schemes is probably closer to three million than to one million. (And even in areas where unemployment is currently low, it has been replaced by a massive increase in part-time, temporary work.)

Every unemployed person 'costs' around £10,000 a year in benefits paid and taxes lost. The Cambridge Journal of Economics shows that one million jobs could be created for £17 billion. This means that, at current taxation levels, an extra £10 million could be raised or saved! Economists also calculate that each employed person annually contributes, on average, around £22,000 to the economy. Therefore, each unemployed person, given a real job, could produce £22,000 worth of production - potentially around £60 billion.

At the same time as we have unemployment, four million workers in Britain work an average of 48 hours a week. This is the lunacy of capitalism. By introducing a 35-hour week with no loss of pay - in other words, sharing out the work - it would be possible to dramatically reduce the number of unemployed whilst simultaneously improving the quality of life for working people.

If this were combined with a massive increase in public services it would be possible to eliminate unemployment. This would allow us to develop a vastly better public transport system, build public housing, and hire more teachers, nursery staff and health workers.

But for the capitalist class profit comes before anything else. So the development of new technology does not mean, as it could, a shorter week for all, but rather longer, backbreaking hours for some and unemployment for the rest.

Marx was right

Capitalism's abject failure to provide the vast bulk of humanity with the material means for a dignified existence is not only due to the greed of individual billionaires or the failure of politicians. If it were, changing society would be a far simpler question of reforming the excesses of capitalism and dealing with the bad apples. But inequality and poverty are part of the fundamental nature of capitalist society.

Over 150 years ago Karl Marx and Friedrich Engels wrote The Communist Manifesto. It has become the most influential political pamphlet of all time. In 1999 a new edition entered the bestsellers list. Marx and Engels were the founders of scientific socialism. In The Communist Manifesto, and later works such as Marx's Capital, they were the first to give a thorough and scientific analysis of the laws and workings of capitalist society: why it results in the polarisation of wealth and, vitally, how it can be overthrown.

one of countless statues in the former stalinist states erected to marx and engels - alien to every thing they argued and fought for. The graffiti reads "we are innocent"

In the last few years their ideas have been regaining popularity. At the end of 1999 Marx was voted the 'greatest thinker of the millennium' in a BBC online poll. Even some capitalist commentators and Wall Street traders have reread Marx and realised how clearly he described capitalism as it is today.

The journalist, Francis Wheen, wrote in his biography of Marx: "The more I studied Marx, the more astoundingly topical he seemed to be. Today's pundits and politicians who fancy themselves as modern thinkers like to mention the buzz-word 'globalisation' at every opportunity - without realising that Marx was already on the case in 1848. The globe-straddling dominance of McDonald's and MTV would not have surprised him in the least."

Even the right-wing tabloid, the Sun, felt impelled to declare in an editorial that "Marx was right". Marx's ideas are, of course, not new. However, for us the important question has to be: are they outmoded, or do they accurately describe the world as it exists today? We would argue that the fundamental tenets of Marx's ideas are as applicable today as ever. Despite the age of Marx and Engels' theories, they are thoroughly modern.

This does not mean that everything they wrote in the 19th century was correct in every detail or has been confirmed by events. On timing and the proximity of the socialist revolution and on some other issues they were mistaken. Many of the demands drawn up in 1848 are now obsolete. Moreover, society today is in many ways very different to then. Nonetheless, an amazing amount of what they formulated about society is as relevant today as when it was written.

It is the economic crisis of capitalism internationally that has forced many commentators to reassess their view of Marx. In January 2001, Time Magazine had a front cover depicting the economic crisis that was bearing down on the US. The headline was, Here Comes the Slump. Their main feature commented: "Karl Marx theorised that capitalism was condemned to repeat depressions because of 'cycles of overproduction'." It concluded by saying that if Marx viewed the US economy in the first week of January he would "no doubt have felt vindicated".

Reality has hit some commentators between the eyes and has forced them to partially recognise Marx's analysis of the nature of capitalist crises which, he explained, were intrinsic to the system. Capitalism is a cyclical system: crises can be triggered by a number of factors, such as financial crashes or political unrest. However, the underlying reasons for crisis are the fundamental contradictions of capitalism as first described by Marx. These include the antagonism between the social, collective nature of production on the one hand, and private ownership of the means of production on the other; and the antagonism between the world market and the limitations of the nation state. Capitalism is based on production for profit and not for social need. The working class creates new value but receives only a portion of that new value back as wages. The capitalists take the rest – the surplus.

protests erupt in argentina - the reality of capitalism

As a result, the working class collectively cannot afford to buy back all the goods it produces. The capitalists partially solve this by ploughing a proportion of the surplus back into industry, but this results in the production of more goods which, at a certain point, actually intensifies the problem. The inevitable results are crises of overproduction and overcapacity. In the long term, the capitalists cannot overcome this problem. As a result, capitalism is a system riven by crisis.

While some commentators have accepted that Marx predicted the fundamental features of the modern economy remarkably well, in general they shy away from the conclusions that he drew. Marx famously declared: "Philosophers have only interpreted the world, the point, however, is to change it."

This does not mean that Marx saw nothing positive in capitalism. He recognised that capitalism, despite all its brutality, played a necessary historic role in developing the productive forces and the world market. It was therefore an advance from the feudal societies that preceded it. Today, the idea of capitalism as a progressive force is unthinkable to most of those involved in the anti-capitalist movement. Yet capitalism has developed the world market and the enormous wealth, science and technique that have laid the foundations for a socialist society.

Under capitalism, however, wealth and power have always been concentrated in the hands of a minority – the capitalists. And the development of technology is not driven by any rational means but by the need for profit. Capitalism is completely incapable of fully harnessing the productive forces it has brought into being. This is a system where science and technique are only ever used partially and inadequately. And the anarchy of the capitalist market always results in increasing wealth and power for a few alongside poverty for the many.

The capitalist class

As Marx explained, the capitalists are those who own the means of production. They own the factories, banks and offices. Marx's prediction that capitalism would lead to an ever-increasing concentration of wealth in the hands of a tiny minority and the increased exploitation of the vast majority worldwide is graphically borne out by the reality at the beginning of the 21st century.

Today the capitalists are a far wealthier and a far smaller class than they were in Marx's time. Capital has been concentrated in fewer and fewer hands at the same time as it has grown beyond the wildest dreams of the Victorian capitalists. In the last 50 years the wealth gap between the richest 20% of humanity and the poorest 20% doubled. Individual multinational companies have become richer than entire countries. The world's 100 biggest companies now control 70% of global trade. Any one of them sells more than any of the poorest 120 countries on the world export market, while 23 of the most powerful sell more than even semi-developed countries such as India, Brazil, Indonesia or Mexico.

The working class sells its ability to work to these people who maximise their profits by paying as little as they can get away with. As far as the capitalists are concerned, as long as we have enough to live on and can ensure that our children - future generations of workers - survive, we have plenty.

In many countries of the world that is all that workers get - enough for a bowl of rice and a floor to sleep on at night. In Britain, over many decades, workers have won more than that - the right to join a trade union, to vote, a National Health Service. However, the capitalists use any chance they get to try and take these things away from us. Anyone who has lived in Britain over the last 20 years knows that. Year after year our living standards have been eroded by cuts in healthcare, education and benefits, longer working hours and worse pay. Like acid on metal, the drip, drip of cuts has eaten away at our standards of living and turned us into one of the poorest working classes in Western Europe.

Commodities

Marx explained that capitalism is the first society based on the mass production of commodities. In previous feudal societies goods were produced by individuals or families, primarily for the use of their lords and masters, as well as for their own personal use. Any production of goods for sale was on a small scale. By contrast, under capitalism, goods (commodities) are mass-produced on machinery owned by the capitalist class. The capitalist class does not make commodities itself, it pays the working class to do that. The commodities produced then enter a process of exchange in which the capitalists attempt to sell them to make a profit. Under this system, market relations dominate every aspect of our lives. In other words, the inner logic of capitalism is that everything – even art, literature, sex and sport – becomes a commodity to be bought and sold.

There are those who argue that this is no longer wholly true. For example, in her book No Logo, the anti-capitalist Naomi Klein seems to argue that the multinationals now sell 'brands' and 'lifestyles' rather than simply selling commodities as they did in the past.

It is true that the huge multinationals such as Nike and McDonald's spend vast sums promoting their brand images. However, no matter how overwhelming the advertising, their aim remains the same as it did in the past - to sell commodities. They use brand image to secure a bigger share of the market than rival products, but if McDonald's or Nike stopped selling burgers or trainers they would still go bust.

Marx explained that the underlying value of commodities is determined by the amount of 'socially necessary human labour' used to produce them. Of course, he understood that the reality of the market is far more complicated than that. Supply and demand, shortages and overabundance all mean that the prices of commodities fluctuate around the underlying value. Nonetheless, it is the labour of the working class which ultimately determines the value of all commodities.

How is the working class exploited?

All workers sell their labour power. This is a commodity to be bought and sold like any other. We receive a certain sum of wages in return for selling our time. How is the value of labour determined? Why does a manager receive more than a secretary? Who decides what a journalist is paid, or a checkout worker, or a bricklayer? The answer is horrifyingly simple: the value of 40 hours' labour is decided in the same way as the value of anything else. It depends on what it costs to produce 40 hours of labour!

What does that mean? It means what it costs to keep a man or woman in a fit state to do 40 hours' work. In other words, if an employer wants those hours worked, he or she has to pay enough to produce those 40 hours of labour or, to be more exact, enough to produce a man or a woman capable of performing it. Skilled workers are paid more simply because it costs more to 'produce' them – to train them to do their job.

As with any other commodity, supply and demand means that the price of labour fluctuates around its underlying value. At bottom, however, the capitalists have to pay enough for a man or woman who is capable of doing the job to live on and to bring up children to do the work for the next generation. From the bosses' point of view, why pay more than this? Why pay more than enough to secure a supply of the commodity required? In fact, employers would probably not be able to pay more even if they wanted to because someone else would pay less and undercut them. Capitalists can only be forced to pay more by the collective struggle of the working class.

Labour is like, but also unlike, other commodities. It is different in that labour creates new commodities and new value. For the capitalist it is like the goose that lays the golden egg. This, Marx argued, is the root of the exploitation of the working class. The working class is never paid the full value of its labour. The capitalists pay workers what is necessary for our survival, what Marx called 'necessary-product'. The rest, which the capitalists expropriate, is called 'surplus-product'.

How much goes to the worker and how much to the capitalists is not fixed. It is a living struggle between the classes. Speed-ups, increasing working hours, cutting tea breaks, stopping bonuses, and the introduction of performance-related pay, all result in the boss getting a larger proportion of the surplus product. On the other side, cuts in the working week and improvements in pay or working conditions increase the workers' share of the surplus product.

What is the working class?

Today it is fashionable to assert that the working class no longer exists. New Labour claims that we will soon all be middle class. So-called 'experts' on the economy talk about how we now live in a knowledge-based society where all you need is access to the internet to escape from membership of the working class.

The truth is very different. In reality, Britain is returning to an 'Upstairs, Downstairs' economy, more akin to the Victorian era. The fastest growing sector of the labour market belongs to those who clean, shop, child mind or garden for others. Low wages and long hours are the norm for working-class people. More and more workers have to take on several jobs just to survive.

As one journalist stated in The Guardian on 6 June 2000: "For those on rock bottom wages, both parents need to work all the hours they can to keep the family afloat financially. Karl Marx would recognise their situation even though the job descriptions may be unfamiliar."

When Marx talked about the working class he did not simply mean people who wore flat caps or the equivalent stereotype in the 19th century. He defined classes not by a superficial façade (what kind of car someone owns or whether their house is pebble-dashed) but by both an economic and a social definition. In Marx's day the average worker was more likely to sell their ability to work in a factory. Today in Britain, millions still work in factories but there are others working in different fields who, nonetheless, produce new value. Others again do not strictly fit this category but are part of the working class because of their social outlook and their economic situation – their wage level and standard of living, etc.

Contrary to popular opinion among the chattering classes, the working class is not disappearing. In fact, it is objectively stronger than it was in Marx's day. When Marx and Engels were writing the working class was a minority worldwide. The working class was growing but large sections of the population were still artisans, small shopkeepers, peasants, and small-business people.

Now, in Britain and other economically advanced countries, those of us who rely on wages make up the overwhelming majority. Of course, some people – the unemployed, pensioners and many single parents – have to survive on the meagre pittance provided by state benefits. They are still members of the working class and the only way they can hope to improve their living standards above the breadline is to work.

Work is the only option available to most of us. In general, stories of individuals

pensioners protest

becoming rich by setting up companies in their bedrooms are a myth. The saga of the dotcoms, where young entrepreneurs believed they had discovered a new way of making millions from the internet, demonstrates this. Even prior to the dotcom bubble bursting, the reality was very different to the fiction. Most internet millionaires, such as Martha Lane-Fox of lastminute.com, are the sons and daughters of existing 'traditional' millionaires. In many cases, less privileged small-business men and women are seeing their companies crushed under the juggernauts of the multinational companies. In 2000, 43,365 small businesses went bust. This is a record figure for a boom year. Up and down the country local high streets are dying because the small shops cannot compete with Tesco, Asda and all the rest.

Capitalism has led to the concentration of wealth and power in ever decreasing numbers of hands at the top. Meanwhile at the bottom, more and more previously middle-class people are forced downwards into the ranks of the working class. This process is taking place in a particularly harsh and barbaric way in Argentina. The heart-rending economic crisis is devastating the lives of the population. The Financial Times declared that "Argentina can no longer afford its middle class" and it is, in fact, rapidly disappearing. The shanty towns are strewn with banners marked 'welcome middle classes' as teachers, lecturers, and bank workers are forced into the ghetto.

In Britain, nothing so dramatic is taking place. Nonetheless, many sections of the population - such as teachers, civil servants and lecturers – who were relatively privileged in the past and who saw themselves as middle class, are now low paid, overworked and increasingly see themselves as part of the working class. They are also beginning to draw the conclusion that the only way they can defend their pay and conditions is to use the traditional weapon of the working class, by taking strike action.

Immediately after New Labour declared that 'we are all middle class now', a Daily Mirror poll showed that 60% of people described themselves as working class - a far higher percentage than was the case even ten years ago. In Britain, 28 million people work for wages, selling our ability to work, our labour power. We are potentially by far the strongest force in British society, and far stronger than in Marx's day.

It is true that the working class has not made its strength felt in Britain over the last few years. However, this does not primarily stem from an objective weakening of its latent power. It is more a result of subjective reasons that can be summed up as a temporarily debilitating lack of confidence. This followed the defeats that the working class suffered during the 1980s and 1990s internationally, and specifically in Britain where the Tory government inflicted a number of blows against the workers' movement. These factors resulted in a low level of class struggles over the last decade.

This has had some objective effects. Sections of the older generation have been affected by the memory of bitter defeats. The younger generation has, in general, no experience of struggle and so is, as yet, inexperienced, raw and untutored. At the same time, right-wing trade union leaders took advantage of the situation to try and entrench their power and detach themselves as far as possible from their members. But like a natural athlete who is a little out of shape through lack of practise, the British working class has not lost its capacity to fight. It only needs to experience its strength in struggle to regain confidence. As it does so, it will also turn on the right-wing union leaders. The first steps in this direction are already underway, as shown by the recent election of left-wing general secretaries in the RMT (rail and maritime workers union), the PCS (civil servants union), and the defeat of Sir Ken Jackson in the AEEU (engineering union).

It is true, however, that the most powerful sections of the working class - that is, the industrial working class whose strength stems from the fact that it is largely responsible for the creation of new value - are a smaller proportion of the workforce now than they were 20 or 30 years ago. The major reason for this is the chronic weakness of British capitalism combined with the conscious policy of Thatcher and her cohorts of moving away from manufacturing to services to undermine the strength of the British working class.

There are other additional, international trends which also had an effect. The major one is capitalism's constant drive to speed up production, creating factories with the capacity to produce ever more commodities. At the same time, capitalism is incapable of fully using the capacity that has been created because, ultimately, the working class cannot afford to buy all of the goods it produces. This leads to overproduction and overcapacity. The bosses attempt to deal with this through lay-offs and downsizing, resulting in a smaller number of industrial workers producing the same amount of commodities that a larger number produced in the past.

In the last 20 years there has been a sevenfold increase in the sales of the biggest multinational companies, yet the number of people they employ has remained virtually the same. (This gives a glimpse of the potential for a democratically planned economy to fully utilise and further develop the productive forces capitalism has created.)

Whilst it is smaller than it was at the height of the post-war economic upswing, however, the industrial working class has far greater numbers today than it did a century ago. In the 24 leading economies, it numbered 51.7 million in 1900, 88 million in 1950, 120 million in 1971 and even in 1998 still numbered 112.8 million. In the US there were 8.8 million industrial workers in 1900, 20.6 million in 1950, 26 million in 1971 and 31 million in 1998.[9]

The decrease in the size of the industrial working class in Britain is also, partially, the result of the international phenomenon known as 'globalisation'. The capitalists in the US, Europe and Japan, in an attempt to restore their profit levels, have set out to drive down the living conditions of the working class. One means by which they have achieved this is by moving production to other countries where labour is cheaper. Nonetheless, the majority of manufacturing industry is still concentrated in the advanced capitalist countries. For example, if the industrial economy of the whole western hemisphere is given the value of 100%, then the US accounts for 76% of this. By contrast, the biggest of the Latin American countries, Brazil, is only 8%.[10]

And while all of the factors mentioned above have had some effect, the strength of the British working class remains immense. The London Underground and rail strikes have given a glimpse of how capitalism can be paralysed when a key section of workers takes action. Even less powerful sections of workers are able to have an effect on the profits of the capitalists. For example, to a far greater degree than in the past, if teachers were to take national strike action millions of parents would be unable to work because of childcare commitments. This would exert real pressure on the capitalist class.

Alienation

Marx did not reduce his analysis of the exploitation of the working class to a simple question of economic poverty alone. He explained that in a capitalist society workers are alienated from the work they do. Hours spent every day building a palace or tarmacking a road are not undertaken for the satisfaction of making something useful or beautiful, but to receive a wage on which to survive. Marx wrote: "And the worker, who for twelve hours weaves, spins, drills, turns, builds, shovels, breaks stones, carries loads etc. - does he [or she] hold this twelve hours' weaving, spinning, drilling, turning, building, shovelling, stone breaking to be a manifestation of his life, as life? On the contrary, life begins for him where this activity ceases, at the table, in the public house, in bed. The twelve hours labour has no meaning for him as weaving, spinning, drilling, etc, but as earnings, which bring him to the table, to the public house, into bed. If the silk worm were to spin in order to continue its existence as a caterpillar, it would be a complete wage-worker."[11]

This description of working life would apply just as much to the workers in McDonald's, Tesco, call centres, on modern building sites or in factories, as it ever did to the weavers and labourers Marx was describing. Instead of making life easier, the increase in automation has reduced ever more jobs to mind-numbing repetition and boredom.

It is not only work that is dehumanising under capitalism. The commodification of human existence – a society where everything is for sale - is deeply alienating. Marx talked about how, in its drive to sell ever new commodities, capitalism created "imaginary appetites" long before TV started to bombard us constantly with a

mcjobs - mcinteresting

thousand new products that claim to keep us young and beautiful, or that we 'must' own to keep up with the Joneses. And long before having the right mobile phone or pair of trainers became a major pressure on almost every young person's existence!

As capitalism has become more brutal over the last 20 years, alienation has undoubtedly increased. Without exaggerating, there is a small section of young people in Britain for whom the system has offered nothing and who are, as a result, almost entirely alienated from society. Work is alienating but it also brings with it the experience of being part of a collective workforce that, potentially at any rate, has the power to fight back. In the organisation of the working class the germ of a new society exists. At times when class struggle is at a high level it tends to increase the sense of common interest and community amongst wide sections of the working class.

One of the worst of all experiences in capitalist Britain is to be a young person who cannot get work – to have been thrown on the scrap heap before your teens are even over. These young people do not even have the right to claim benefits until they are 18 years old. They are surrounded by the pressures and demands of modern capitalist culture – that to fit in they have to own clothes and trainers costing hundreds of pounds - yet they often have no income at all. There are now generations of such young people who have grown up in the 1980s and 1990s on the housing estates throughout Britain. The result has been an increase in street crime and robbery, almost all of it carried out against people who are also living in poverty. There has also been an increase in drug addiction: for example, a 400% increase in the number of children who died from sniffing gas and glue between 1980 and 1990.[12] The reasons for drug use are wide and varied. Nonetheless, the increase in every kind of drug addiction and dependency, both legal and illegal, is primarily a result of a more alienated society.

This increase in alienation is a direct result of neo-liberal policies. This is graphically illustrated by the experience of the ex-mining villages around the country. The defeat of the 1984-85 miners' strike and the closure of the pits have left previously strong communities suffering the ravages of unemployment, poverty and drug addiction.

As long as we live in a capitalist society then, as Marx described, "brutalisation" and "moral degradation" will remain. However, future action by working-class people – both in the workplaces and communities – will to a degree counter the current trend. A new generation will see the point of collective struggle. One strand of future mass campaigns will undoubtedly be the struggle to strengthen our communities and to prevent anti-social crime. These will have nothing in common with Blair's empty moralising about being "tough on crime, tough on the causes of crime", whilst simultaneously exacerbating the causes of crime with cuts and more cuts. On the contrary, campaigns against anti-social crime in working-class communities should be linked to demands for decent jobs, facilities for young people and the right to claim benefits.

Is Marx relevant in the 21st century?

According to New Labour, theories developed in the dark, satanic mills of the Victorian era are no longer relevant. It claims that there are good and bad bosses (mostly good). If we are 'reasonable', 'patient' and 'hard working' we can convince good bosses to pay us well. Yet the experience of working people and the statistics - even the government's statistics - show that this is absolutely untrue.

In the two decades after the second world war capitalism developed at a rapid pace. (This was possible because of exceptional and unrepeatable circumstances following the war, when whole swathes of Europe had been reduced to rubble.) It was in those post-war years that workers in the West won many of the benefits, such as the welfare state, that are being constantly eroded today. In the early 1970s capitalism went into crisis internationally. Since then the capitalists have set about restoring their profits to the level of the post-war years. They have done this primarily by driving down the wages of the working class, in other words, by increasing their own share of the surplus product.

In the US, the most powerful economy in the world, the longest boom in its history has recently come to a close. Yet, even at the height of the boom - in 1999 - 80% of the population were no better off than they were 20 years ago and 50 million people (nearly 20%) were worse off.

Meanwhile, the capitalist class is drowning in riches. According to the US magazine, Business Week, if a US worker who earned $25,000 (£16,500) in 1994 received the same percentage income increase as the average boss over the same period he or she would now be earning $138,350. The US, the world's only superpower, contains the most extreme polarisation of wealth. On the one hand, it is normal for chief executives to receive phenomenal sums in bonuses - like the $45 million (£30 million) that Wendt received from Consecso Insurance just for turning up at his new job. However, the income of individual chief executives is chicken feed compared with the wealth and power of the owners of the big corporations. Two US corporations alone - General Motors and Ford - exceed the Gross Domestic Product (GDP) of the whole of sub-Saharan Africa. In glaring contradiction with this unimaginable wealth the US also contains ever-increasing poverty: 0.5% of the population of the USA own as much as the bottom 90%.

But the US is only the leader in what is an international trend. In 2000 there were seven million people worldwide with liquid assets of more than $1 million - an increase of 18% in one year alone. In Britain the average income of a chief executive of a FTSE 100 company is a huge £643,000 a year. This means, by the way, that all but the most obese are literally worth their weight in gold!

New Labour argues that these individuals 'earn' their wealth with their talent and entrepreneurial skills. Yet in Britain there are a mere 392 people who sit on the remuneration boards adjudicating on the pay and bonuses of the top company directors of the 98 largest companies. Thirty directors sit on more than one remuneration board. This is a tiny club of wealthy people deciding how much more gold to heap on themselves and their friends and relatives. There were 6,600 millionaires in 1992 and now there are more than 47,000.

By contrast, as the house journal of the financial wing of the British ruling class, The Financial Times, commented: "Wage inequality is greater than for 100 years... one in two less-skilled men is without work, and one in five households lack access to an earned income." Employment insecurity for those who do have jobs is at "the highest level for 30 years", according to the Joseph Rowntree Foundation.

All the neo-liberal attacks on the living standards of the working class have been designed, at base, to increase the ruling class's share of surplus value at the expense of the working class. This has been achieved by decreasing the 'social wage' - cutting the welfare state. But it has also been carried out directly on the factory floor. Today the bosses take a much larger percentage of the surplus created by the working class than was the case in the recent past. As the American economist William

Greider explains: "In 1975, an average American family needed 18 weeks of earnings to buy an average-priced car; by 1995 the cost of the new car consumed 28 weeks of income."[13]

Globalisation

This example is based on US car workers. Yet, many car plants internationally have been moved away from the US and Europe to areas where labour is far cheaper, such as Latin America and Eastern Europe. The same has happened in many other sectors. Greider describes the reasons why: "American garment workers could make a shirt with 14 minutes human labour, while it took 25 minutes in Bangladesh. But the average US wage was $7.53 an hour, while in Bangladesh it was 25 cents, an edge that would not be erased even if the Bangladeshi wages were doubled or quadrupled. Or steel: US industry required 3.4 hours of human labour to produce a ton of steel, while Brazil took 5.8 hours. But wages difference was 10 to 1: $13 an hou

This demonstrates one of the ways in which the bosses were able to hugely increase their profits by lowering wages in the 1990s. However, in doing so they have also massively exacerbated the problems that the capitalist system is facing now, and will face in the future.

The coming crisis

Until recently the US economy was booming. Like Atlas it held up the world economy. This was a boom that massively intensified the inequalities of capitalism. It was also the precursor to recession: in the 12 months up to March 2002, US big-business profits suffered the biggest drop since the Great Depression of the 1930s. Despite this, at the beginning of 2002 most commentators were claiming that the US economy was on the road to recovery. As the collapse of WorldCom and the slide on the stock markets show, this was more than a little over-optimistic.

Capitalism is a cyclical system and the current recession will, at a certain stage, come to an end, but the underlying systemic malaise will remain. Economic stagnation, mass unemployment and underemployment, and the general undermining of working peoples' living standards, are all capitalism has to offer in the 21st century. The most modern understanding of can be found in the writings of Marx.

Today the capitalists claim to have solved overproduction with techniques like 'just-in-time' production. Yet only a few years ago, massive overproduction was the major factor in the South-East Asian economic crisis which has decimated the living standards of the working class of the area. Overproduction is also at the root of the

tube and train strikes as workers are forced to fightback

current international crisis. After 1997 the US was able to temporarily ameliorate the situation by acting as the 'buyer of last resort' for the world's goods. This is now coming to an end.

Even in instances where overproduction has been partially overcome, it is replaced by a crisis of overcapacity. That is when capitalism is only able to function by leaving a large proportion of productive capacity idle. In the European car market there was a massive 40% overcapacity in 1999. This has been the primary reason for the merger mania that has swept the world car industry. In the full knowledge that some factories will have to close and some firms go to the wall, the world's car producers are slogging it out for markets in a fight to the death. This is what lay behind the mass slashing of jobs at Ford Dagenham, Vauxhall Luton and Longbridge.

The method by which the capitalists have restored their profits in the 1990s has laid the seeds for a catastrophic crisis. They have driven down the wages of workers in the West whilst simultaneously moving production to the ex-colonial countries where labour is cheaper. Inevitably, this is exacerbating the problems of overproduction and overcapacity. On a global scale the working class receives a considerably smaller share of the value it creates. Therefore, it can buy back only a smaller percentage of the goods it produces. In the current economic crisis the capitalists' chickens are coming home to roost.

An additional factor in the 1990s US boom has been the massive overvaluation of stock markets throughout the world, but particularly in the US itself. This has been combined with a huge expansion of credit – or, as it is otherwise known, debt. In 1999 private savings in the US went negative for the first time since the 1930s. In 2000 the total private-sector debt was around 130% of GDP, compared with less than 100% in 1929 when the stock market crash on Wall Street heralded the Great Depression of the 1930s. Credit, like elastic, can be stretched so far. At a certain point, however, it will have to snap back into line with reality. The result is the collapse of companies like Enron and WorldCom as the 'astute' business practises of the 1990s are revealed as the reckless gambling of a terminally short-sighted capitalist class.

But capitalism's crises never affect only the billionaires and Wall Street traders. In fact in 2001, despite the world economic downturn, the number of millionaires still increased by 3%! The 'masters of the universe' may suffer a bit of a hangover as a result of their decade-long Wall Street party, but it is working people and the poor who will really feel the consequences.

Britain - the world's biggest hedge fund

B ritain, the world's first capitalist superpower, is now the puny relative of the heavyweight capitalist countries. Like a little leaky boat caught in the backwash from an ocean liner, Britain is buffeted by the fortunes of the major powers - above all those of the US.

British manufacturing industry is in catastrophic decline. Manufacturing remains the base of any modern economy because it is primarily responsible for the creation of new value. In 1978 this sector employed seven million people, almost three times as many as in financial services. Today only 4.3 million are employed in manufacturing while the service sector employs 5.2 million.

Britain has become the sweatshop of Europe. The majority of the remaining manufacturing workers are working for overseas firms which are exploiting some of the cheapest labour in the European trading bloc. In 1999 Britain was producing more cars than at any time since the 1960s – before the pull-outs by BMW, Vauxhall

demonstrating for a living wage

and Ford – yet less than one-hundredth of its output was by British-owned companies. Britain is also the leading producer of TVs in Europe. But of the six companies that manufacture them, five are Japanese and one is Korean.

This leaves Britain exceptionally vulnerable to the vagaries of the world economy. As the 1997-98 world economic crisis graphically illustrated, when a company is in trouble it tends to close its plants abroad before those at home. The result was the closure of Siemens in the North-East of England, along with other major job losses, especially in Scotland. The same point is demonstrated by the car industry where chronic overproduction has led to workers facing huge job losses at almost all of Britain's car plants. In a future serious economic crisis the flight of foreign investors to their own markets will be far more severe than even that which we have already experienced.

For while globalisation has transformed the planet, it has also come up against definite limits, especially the barriers of the nation state (such as tariffs, borders and currencies, etc). The nation state is part of the fundamental structure of capitalism and, as long as capitalism remains, it will never be more than partially overcome. There is virtually no such a thing as a genuinely transnational company – that is, a company with no 'home' nation. The closest that exists is Shell, whose ownership is based in two countries, the Netherlands and Britain. John Gray points out in his book, False Dawn: The Delusions of Global Capitalism, that the multinationals are not "homeless transnational institutions which move across borders without cost and express no particular national business culture. They are often companies which retain strong roots in their original economies and cultures. In a systematic and comprehensive survey, Ruigrok and van Tulder concluded that few, if any, of the world's biggest companies are fully global... Nearly all multinationals express and embody a single parent national culture." In other words, the multinationals have a home nation to which they tend to return when times get hard. The weakness of British capitalism means that very few multinationals are British owned. The few that are reached prominence decades or even centuries ago. All but two of the top ten British multinationals are based on 'old' industry, in most cases raw materials such as oil.[14]

Longest hours in Europe

In the 1970s the weakness of British capitalism used to be put down to the 'greedy workers'. Today few dare to raise this idea seriously. British workers work the longest hours in the European Union. The average British household now works seven hours a week longer than it did at the start of the 1980s. Longer working hours have meant that the average night's sleep in Britain is now down to seven hours, compared to nine at the beginning of the last century.

*demonstrating against low pay - women workers in Britain,
as worldwide face the brunt of robbing bosses*

Regardless of the ever-increasing workload shouldered by working people, industry is in an increasingly decrepit state. The reality is that the ruling class in Britain no longer invests in industry. It is an increasingly parasitic class, driven by its own short-term interests. Productivity levels (the average amount produced per hour by each worker) languish behind the rest of the so-called 'advanced' world. A recent study by the London School of Economics showed that if productivity levels in Britain were given a score of 100, France would score 133, followed by Germany on 129, with the US on 126. Francis Green, professor of economics at Kent University explained: "There is a satiation point at which productivity growth needs to rely on modernising industry through investment rather than further work intensification."[15]

The capitalist class has always been driven by the need to make profits. Today, however, the long-term crisis of British capitalism has resulted in a ruling class which is, in the main, exceptionally short-sighted and driven purely by the best way to make a quick buck. Overwhelmingly, productivity increases have come not as a result of new technology but from the increased exploitation of working people. Research and development in industry has been lower than the rest of Europe for 20 years. It has recently fallen even further, from 2.29% of GDP in 1986 to 1.94% in 1996. In 1999 investment in British manufacturing plummeted by a further 13.6%.

Yet in 2000, according to the government's figures, Britain became the fourth-largest economy in the world in terms of income. This growth comes mainly from the finance sector and from massive investments of British capitalism abroad. This has been fuelled by the huge profits from North Sea oil. Rather than these profits being reinvested to increase industrial capacity, they have been used to cushion the effects of Thatcher's catastrophic policies of mass unemployment in the 1980s. And they have also been used by British capitalism to invest abroad, particularly in buying assets in the US economy.

"The world's biggest hedge fund" was how a recent report by the City firm, Smithers & Co, described Britain. In other words, it is just one big casino where the world's financiers come and gamble their billions. The report went on to say that Britain was uniquely vulnerable to a world recession because its "foreign liabilities exceed its assets and it is only remaining profitable by making skilful bets on the financial markets". This remains true even though, at the time of writing, Britain has not yet been as badly affected by the current US downturn as other countries – ironically because the devastated manufacturing industry is such a small sector in the British economy.

The finance sector is in a position of overweening dominance over the economy as a whole. The City of London is second only to New York and Tokyo in its international importance. However, even finance capital is not actually dominated by the feeble British bosses. The London Stock Exchange (LSE) is under serious threat of takeover. The Guardian accidentally revealed how incompetent it believes British big business to be in an editorial: "But why should the LSE be any different from a metal basher in the West Midlands or indeed from City banks that are now owned by the Germans, the Americans and the Dutch? There are no questions of national economic sovereignty involved here, and if the LSE falls into the hands of the Swedes, then so be it. If it does not, the LSE will be able to strike a better deal with Frankfurt. Whatever happens, the stock market is bound to be run better than it was before."[16]

For working-class people the pathetic weakness of British capitalism has already meant decades of increasing hardship. Unfortunately, in future economic crises, we will once again suffer the consequences of the British ruling class's enfeebled state.

How could socialism work ?

I n the 300 years or so of its existence capitalism has transformed the planet over and over again. Rail, electricity, the internal combustion engine, flight, space travel, telephones and electronic computers, the list is endless. The world economy is 17 times the size it was a century ago. In 1900 there were only a few thousand cars worldwide. Now there are 501 million. Engineers built the first electronic computers in the early 1940s. In 1949, Popular Mechanics magazine predicted that "computers in the future may have only 1,000 tubes and weigh only one and a half tonnes".[1] Today the smallest laptop can process more data than the most powerful computers in the world 50 years ago.

Despite this, all the technology developed by capitalism has not provided clean water for 1.2 billion people or food for the 841 million who are seriously malnourished. Nor has it prevented the Aids epidemic rampaging through Africa. Upwards of 28 million Africans have the HIV virus and only 30,000 of them can get treatment. Capitalism is capable of spending billions on developing weaponry that is used to

south african trade unionists demonstrate against profiteering drugs companies

bomb the poor of Afghanistan into the rubble, but it cannot solve poverty, hunger or disease.

And capitalism is threatening the very future existence of the planet. Scientists predict that, as a result of global warming, sea levels are likely to rise by up to one metre this century. This would devastate the inhabitants of the flood plains of Bangladesh and Egypt, and worldwide hundreds of millions of the very poor would be displaced. Even these figures are probably conservative as they are based on estimates made in the 1980s. The latest surveys indicate that the situation could be more severe as they report that Arctic sea ice has thinned by 40% in the last three decades.

Capitalism has enormously developed the productive forces but it is controlled by the unplanned and blind play of those very productive forces. It is a system where the only driving force is the need to maximise profits.

William Greider begins his book on modern capitalism by describing the system: "A wondrous new machine, strong and supple, a machine that reaps as it destroys... Now imagine that there are skilful hands on board, but no one is at the wheel. In fact, this machine has no wheel or any internal governor to control the speed and direction. It is sustained by its own forward motion, guided mainly by its own appetites."[18]

Under capitalism it is the blind forces of profiteering that are in the driving seat. Governments bow down before the rule of capital unless they are prepared to challenge it. Nowhere is this clearer than on the issue of the environment. Every so often the world's leaders come together to plan how to 'save the planet'. They come up with targets to limit damage to the environment. The largest and most powerful economy on earth, the US, always manages to get the targets lowered. For example, scientists agree that releases of carbon dioxide and other greenhouse gases need to be cut by at least 60%. Yet all that has been agreed by governments internationally is a minimal reduction to the levels of 1990. Even this modest goal is hedged about with ways of bending the rules. For example, countries are allocated targets for carbon emissions. Russia has far lower carbon emissions than its target figure. This has nothing to do with measures to help the environment but is purely because of the catastrophic collapse of the Russian economy since the fall of Stalinism in the former Soviet Union a decade ago. Under the rules, Russia is able to sell its resulting 'carbon credits' to other countries – which then use them to count towards reaching their own target! Even with these attempts to create a system where the rich countries can buy fictional claims of having done their environmental duty, the US – which produces one quarter of the world's greenhouse gases – has refused to sign up. All previous experience shows that even these paltry targets will never be met under capitalism.

Capitalism is incapable of fully harnessing the science and technology it has

somewhere to live? - an environmental and social disaster worldwide

brought into being. It is incapable of providing for the needs of humanity or of protecting our fragile planet. By contrast, a socialist society would be able to harness the enormous potential of human talent and technique in order to build a society and economy which could meet

That does not mean that every problem could be immediately overcome as a result of a socialist government abolishing the rule of capital. Far from it. Removing the profit motive would only be the beginning of building a new society. It is not possible to create socialism in one country surrounded by a world capitalist market, particularly an economically underdeveloped one, as the example of Russia in the last century shows. The leaders of the Russian revolution in 1917 – Lenin, Leon Trotsky and the Bolshevik party – saw the overthrow of capitalism in Russia as the prelude to an international transformation of society. They understood that, economically, Russia was not ready for socialism, but the world was. For them the success or failure of the Soviet Union depended on the working class of other countries successfully overthrowing capitalism.

This is even truer today, given the increased integration of the world economy, than it was in 1917, even for the economically more advanced countries like Britain. Nonetheless, there is an enormous amount that could be achieved by a socialist government in the immediate period after it came to power, as part of a transition from capitalism to socialism. Just cutting the working week to a maximum of 35 hours without loss of pay, or providing free, high-quality childcare for all who wanted it, would transform the lives of millions of people.

Socialist democracy

A socialist economy would have to be a planned economy. This would involve bringing all of the big corporations, which control around 80% of the British economy, into democratic public ownership, under working-class control. Of course, it would not mean bringing small businesses, such as the local shops, many of which are forced out of business by the multinationals, into public ownership. Nor would it mean, as opponents of socialism claim, taking away personal 'private property'. On the contrary, socialists are in favour of everyone having the right to a decent home and the other conveniences of modern life.

A genuine socialist government would not be dictatorial. It would extend and deepen democracy enormously. This would be much more far-reaching than the parliamentary democracies of capitalism where we simply get to vote every few years for MPs who do whatever they like once elected. Instead, everyone would get to take part in deciding how society and the economy would be run. Nationally, regionally and locally – at every level - elected representatives would be accountable and subject to instant recall. Therefore, if the people who had elected them did not like what their representative did, they could make them stand for immediate re-election and, if they wished, replace them with someone else.

Elected representatives would also only receive the average wage. Today MPs are a privileged section of society. Their lives are remote from those of ordinary people. This is no accident. From the earliest days of the Labour Party, the ruling class tried to buy-off socialist MPs. Its method is usually subtler than brown envelopes of cash: it is a high salary, a very comfortable lifestyle and the drip, drip of ceaseless flattery about how 'sensible' and 'wise' it is to be 'moderate' and 'realistic'. The result has been that countless numbers of MPs have decided that the best way to emancipate the working class is one by one – starting with themselves.

That is why members of the Socialist Party who become MPs will only take the average wage of a skilled worker. In the 1980s, three MPs (Dave Nellist, Terry Fields and Pat Wall) were elected as Labour MPs on the policies of Militant (the Socialist Party's predecessor). All took a worker's wage. Today Joe Higgins, a TD (MP) in the Irish parliament, and a member of our sister organisation in Ireland, takes a worker's wage and has been described by the tabloid press as "the red that money can't buy". A socialist government would ensure that no elected representatives received financial privileges as a result of their position but, instead, lived the same lifestyle as those they represented.

There is another crucial sense in which democracy would be far fuller in a socialist society. Under capitalism most of the important decisions are not taken in Westminster or local council chambers, they are taken in the boardrooms of the big corporations. By contrast, a socialist government would bring major industry into democratic public ownership. It would be necessary to draw up a plan, involving the whole of society, on what industry needed to produce. At every level, in communities and workplaces, committees would be set up and would elect representatives to regional and national government – again on the basis of recall at anytime if they disagreed with their decisions. Everybody would be able to participate in real decision-making about how best to run society.

Many people will argue that this is utopian, that people would not be bothered to participate in such bodies. Yet in every mass struggle - from the Paris Commune of 1871 onwards - the embryos of this type of structure have come into existence. In Britain during the struggle to defeat the poll tax, when 18 million refused to pay the iniquitous tax, hundreds of thousands of people took part in meetings to plan the campaign. While the anti-poll tax unions were only temporary bodies, organised to fight against a single Tory attack, they nonetheless give a glimpse of working people's capacity to organise.

Even today, thousands of working-class people attend their tenants' associations and other community meetings. And organisations in a workers' state would be completely different to the toothless bodies that working-class people are currently allowed to take part in - the committees would actually have the power to say how the economy and society is organised.

In addition, for a planned economy to work, it would be vital that the working class had the time to take part in the running of society. Therefore, measures such as a shorter working week and decent, affordable childcare would be a prerequisite for society to develop towards socialism.

Another argument against a planned economy is that society is now too complicated to be planned. Some people argue that, in the past, when the majority of people's aspirations were more limited, it may have been possible to plan an economy. But that today, when people want washing machines, videos and fashionable clothes, they claim planning just would not work.

Yet modern technology would, in reality, make planning far easier than it was in the past. In Russia, following the revolution in 1917 - when working-class people took power for the first time - an attempt was made to build a new society in a situation of extreme economic and cultural backwardness. The Russian peoples faced a desperate situation. Many of the most active socialists had been killed fighting the civil war. At the same time, illiteracy was widespread and most workers lacked administrative skills. This meant that in many cases, the soviets (workers' councils) had no choice but to keep on the specialists and administrators of the old absolutist regime, even at the cost of bribing them with privileges. In the town of Vyatka in 1918, for example, no fewer than 4,476 out of 4,766 officials were the same individuals who had previously served the tsar.

The economy of the Soviet Union has been devastated. It was under attack from imperialist armies and was isolated as the world's only workers' state. Under these conditions, the system did degenerate and a hideous bureaucracy developed. The economy was, therefore, a mangled distortion of a planned economy. Decisions, far from being taken by society as a whole, were taken by a few privileged bureaucrats at the top.

Nonetheless, up until the early 1970s the nationalised economies of the Soviet Union and Eastern Europe produced impressive advances, especially in heavy industries, though consumer goods were generally in short supply and of poor quality. Despite their many shortcomings, however, they also provided basic education, healthcare, and other social amenities to the majority of the population. For the Soviet Union, which in 1917 was an extremely economically backward country (something like India today) these were major advances unparalleled in any capitalist country.

The restoration of capitalism in the former Soviet Union has been an unmitigated disaster. The economy has collapsed by 50% and life expectancy has fallen in ten years to the same level it was in the 1950s. The human suffering that has resulted from the reintroduction of capitalism is immense. One small glimpse of it was given by an interview the journalist Robert Fisk conducted with a young Russian woman, Natasha. She was desperate for money and had, like tens of thousands of others, become involved in international prostitution. Fisk suggested to her that she and her friends were victims of "the worst side of men". Natasha disagreed: "They were victims of the collapse of the Soviet Union, she said, a way of life – free schooling, free universities, free apartments – that had been taken from them."[19]

Whilst there was widespread dissatisfaction in the Soviet Union because of the nightmare of Stalinism, at least it provided the basics. In a negative sense, the reintroduction of capitalism has shown how much better a planned economy (even a fatally distorted one) was in providing a far higher standard of living for ordinary people than capitalism has been able to do.

Capitalism today has provided the tools which could enormously aid the genuine, democratic planning of an economy. Firstly, there is a far higher level of education amongst working class people than there was at the beginning of the last century. And capitalism has developed all kinds of technology that could be used to assist in planning. We have the internet, market research, supermarket loyalty cards that record the shopping habits of every customer, and so on. Big business uses this technology to find out what it can sell. Could it not be used rationally instead to find out what people need and want?

In any case, big businesses themselves do plan. Capitalism is an anarchic and blind system. But the big corporations use their own international structures to try and maximise their profits. All the car companies fix the prices of components in their profit-and-loss columns in order to cook the books. Ford uses a huge internet programme to procure the cheapest possible components worldwide.

The multinationals use extensive planning to avoid paying taxes. One study of 200 US corporations found that "the average multinational firm with subsidiaries in more than five regions uses income shifting to reduce its taxes to 51.6% of what they would otherwise be".[20] Similarly, BMW claimed in 1993 that 95% of its profit was made overseas. From 1988-92, BMW reduced its taxes from 545 million deutschmarks to 31 million in this way (from around £200m to £11m).

The general trend of capitalism, with its increasing monopolisation, is towards internal planning. However, under capitalism this process will never be finished. A blind system based on profit and competition will never be able to plan beyond a certain limit. But a socialist government would strengthen and develop the methods of planning currently used to maximise profit and avoid taxes in order to plan society for the benefit of all.

Doesn't the collapse of the Soviet Union show that planning doesn't work?

Leon Trotsky was one of the leaders of the Russian revolution. He went on to lead a heroic fight against the Stalinist degeneration of the Soviet Union. As far back as 1936, Trotsky put forward two alternatives for the Soviet Union: "A successful uprising of the Russian working class, a political revolution and the restoration of democracy, or the return of capitalism with calamitous consequences for the mass of the population." He went on to explain: "The fall of the present dictatorship, if it were not replaced by a new socialist power, would thus mean a return to capitalist relations with a catastrophic decline of industry and culture."[21]

As we have explained, the regimes in the former Soviet Union and Eastern Europe were not genuinely socialist, but a grotesque caricature. This meant that their collapse was inevitable and could only have been prevented if the bureaucracy had been overthrown and replaced by genuine workers' democracy. To work efficiently a planned economy must be based on workers' democracy. Economic planning in Russia and Eastern Europe took the form of central command from above by bureaucratic ministries and managers acting on the orders of the privileged ruling caste. There was not a trace of democracy at any level.

In the early decades of the Soviet Union's existence, and despite the lack of democracy, the economy took huge strides forward. During the 1970s and 1980s, however, it became clear that the outdated, rigid framework of the Stalinist system could not cope either with technological change or the social demands of a much more developed society. Even as the Soviet Union (under its 'leader' Leonid Brezhnev) appeared to reach the pinnacle of its influence as a superpower, degenerative processes were eating away at the foundations. Sections of the bureaucracy, moreover, sensing impending collapse and fearful of losing their material privileges, were ready to abandon 'socialism' and stake their future on a transition to capitalism.

In the 1980s, workers' struggles shook Poland, followed by a mood of mass opposition in East Germany, Hungary, the former Czechoslovakia and elsewhere. This triggered a political avalanche throughout Eastern Europe. Initially, the sweeping mass movements had features of political revolution: workers demanded democratisation of the factories, economic planning and the state. Such was the deep revulsion against the grotesque Stalinist model of 'socialism', however, that progressive demands for democratic advances towards genuine socialism were soon engulfed by a counter-revolutionary tide in favour of 'the market' - that is, capitalism.

The capitalists worldwide have used the collapse of Stalinism to try to discredit socialist ideas and to claw back many of the gains working-class people made in the post-war period, during which Stalinism acted as a certain counterweight to capitalism. The neo-liberal offensive, the return of the naked, unashamed brutality of capitalism, began in the 1980s but has accelerated massively since the Stalinist system fell apart. The capitalists gained a propaganda victory from the collapse of Stalinism. In the longer term, however, their over-confident brutality in the following decade has gone a long way to undermine their system and to encourage a new generation to see the need for an alternative.

Socialism more than sharing out wealth

It is often argued that socialists simply want to share out the wealth. This, it is asserted, would only mean increased misery for the rich - as the wealth would not be enough to obliterate poverty. But we are not interested in merely doing this. Of course, it would be nice to take some of Bill Gates's $36 billion (£24 billion), but in order for socialism to work it would be necessary to do much more than that.

Some of the immediate measures that could be taken include:

1. Eliminating arms spending

The US has promised to rebuild Afghanistan after bombing it to smithereens. Yet the $297 million (£200 million) it has pledged in 2002 is equal to just seven hours of US defence spending.[22] Arms spending has accounted for $1 trillion a year worldwide since the end of the cold war. This alone could provide $1,000 a year for every family on the planet. Just 25% of the cost of president George W Bush's Star

us troops invade afghanistan

Wars programme would provide clean drinking water for the billion people who are currently without it.

2. Sharing out work

Even at the end of the economic boom in the late 1990s there were still 35 million unemployed in the European Union. At the same time, those in work are working longer hours than ever before. This is madness: a socialist government would immediately share out the work (see Chapter Two).

In addition, it would use modern technology to limit the number of hours it was necessary to work. A socialist government could immediately introduce a maximum 35-hour week, with no loss of pay. Capitalism's remorseless drive for profit means that new technology has been used, not to shorten the working week, but to throw workers on the scrap heap. Greider explains: "During the last generation the world's largest multinational corporations have grown sevenfold in sales. Yet the worldwide employment of these global firms has remained virtually flat since the early 1970s, hovering around 26 million people. The major multinationals grew in sales from $721 billion in 1971 to $5.2 trillion in 1991, claiming a steadily growing share of commerce (one third of all manufacturing exports, three quarters of commodity trade, four fifths of the trade in technology and management services). Yet the human labour required for each unit of their output is diminishing dramatically."

There is currently serious overcapacity in almost every sector of the market. As the economist Will Hutton declared in The Observer: "We are living in a world of glut, we have too much of everything from grain to cars." This is the real lunacy of capitalism. We have too much grain - which means more than can be sold at a profit - yet in Africa 20 million people are starving.

A socialist government would harness technology to lower the number of hours it is necessary to work. This would give working-class people more time to participate in running society. Combined with a massive programme of socially necessary projects - such as increasing the numbers of teachers, doctors and nurses - unemployment could be eliminated.

3. Ending competition and duplication

Private ownership of the means of production results in constant duplication. Companies fiercely compete to produce a certain product first and best. Socialism would eliminate this and thereby save a huge amount of resources. There would also be no need for marketing, on which capitalism spends $1 trillion a year. This does not mean, as is commonly claimed, that socialism would result in a lack of choice or poor quality goods: a society where everyone dresses in a grey uniform. It would be possible to have far more choice of the things which people desire to have a variety of (such as clothes, music, holidays etc) than under capitalism. However, society might choose not to have 200 brands of washing powder.

Meeting the needs of humanity and the environment

On the basis of these three measures alone it would be possible to improve living conditions immeasurably in a very short period of time. But the highest stage of socialism means more than that, what Marx called a society of 'superabundance'. This would be a society that truly meets the needs of humanity. Given that we live in a world 30% of which has no electricity, a world where 50% of humanity has never made a phone call, it would take an enormous development of the productive forces to create a society of superabundance.

But does this also suggest that socialism would lead to the destruction of the environment? On the contrary, the fight for socialism is given added urgency because it is the only way of rescuing the world from environmental disaster. Capitalism, in its wanton chaos, is destroying the planet.

That is not to say that socialism would return to a more primitive society. Far from it. Socialism has to further develop technology and science. Two thirds of the world's population live in absolute poverty. Socialists are not interested in sharing out the misery, we want a decent life for all. That requires utilising technological and scientific innovations.

However, there does not have to be a contradiction between this and safeguarding the planet. What is needed if we are to save the world is long-term planning that would be able to develop alternative technologies that did not harm the environment. This could only be achieved on the basis of democratic socialism. Capitalism operates purely on the basis of the profit motive. To increase the price of products by claiming that they are 'environmentally friendly' is one thing, it is quite another to stop environmental devastation. It will never be in the interests, or within the capabilities, of any multinational to plan long term or to put the general needs of humanity for an inhabitable world and safe food above the narrow, short-term need to make a quick profit.

By contrast, a democratically run planned economy would be able to take rational decisions on the basis of aiming to meet the needs of humanity. It would decide what technology to develop and use, what food to produce, and when and where to build, while taking into consideration the need to protect and repair our planet for future generations.

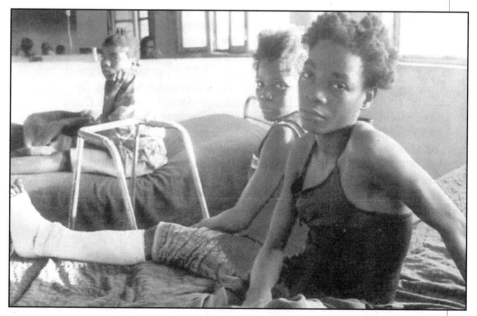

the insanity of capitalism in africa - a hospital without basic supplies in a world of plenty

It is not possible or necessary here and now - amid a society where profit is god and humanity is bent and distorted under its endless dictates – to draw up a full or accurate picture of a socialist society. Future generations, who will be more informed and knowledgeable than us, will do that. But looking objectively, instead of through the dollar-tinted spectacles of big business, only an ingrained pessimist could argue that the replacement of the anarchy of the market with a society based on rational and democratic planning would not be a vast improvement. We can only begin to visualise what science and technique could achieve if they were turned away from making profits for the warmongers and the drug companies and towards the common good.

Nor can we fully imagine how human relations would be lifted onto a higher plane in a new society. But it is possible to see that many of the nightmarish aspects of human relations today are rooted in the society we live in. Any society based on vast inequality will inevitably be divided and prejudiced. The capitalist class needs divisions amongst those they oppress in order to maintain its rule.

For example, racism has been an integral part of capitalism since its infancy when it was used to justify the slave trade. Later, racism was adapted to justify the colonial powers carving up the world between them. Today racism is still ingrained in capitalist society. The increased wealth and privilege of a small minority of black and Asian people is used to disguise the fact that we still live in a deeply unequal society. In the US, the average annual income for a black American is 61% less per year than the average white income. This is the same difference as it was in 1880![23] In Britain, on average, black and Asian workers earn three quarters of the wage of their white counterparts. And black people are five times as likely to be stopped by the police.

Internationally, direct colonial rule may have ended but imperialism still dictates to the poor countries of the world via the multinationals and their agencies – the International Monetary Fund (IMF) and the World Bank. Capitalism is more than happy to adapt the ideology of racism to its own ends whether that it is to justify the nightmare of poverty that is Africa under capitalism, or to distract workers in Britain from the real reasons that our public services are crumbling.

Discrimination against women is also embedded in the structure of capitalism. In Britain the position of women has improved dramatically compared to two generations ago. Nonetheless, although women now make up over 50% of the workforce, on average they still earn only 72% of male wages. Even though most women work they still tend to bear the brunt of domestic tasks. Even when women work full time they spend an average of eight hours a week more than their partner cooking and shopping.[24]

It is not 'natural' or 'inevitable' that women earn less and carry the majority of the domestic load. What is considered 'normal' is determined by the society we live in. The oppression of women is rooted in class society. The way that capitalism is organised and structured – in particular the role that the family has played and still plays as an economic and social unit – perpetuates and reinforces women's oppression.

When ordinary people talk about 'family' they mean real individuals – parents, children, partners. However, under capitalism the family is also a social and economic unit based on the dependence of the 'non-productive' members of the household on an individual wage earner (traditionally the man). The family plays an ideological and an economic role. It is used to discipline and socialise young people, and to prepare them for their given role in capitalist society. It is also used to reinforce the idea of bearing personal responsibility for society's ills.

When Thatcher said that "there is no such thing as society", only the family and individuals, she also said that the family was a "building block". In doing so she summed up the attitude of capitalism to the family. Thatcher believed that it was the duty of the family to bear the burden of looking after children, the sick and the elderly. Conveniently, this meant that she could cut back on the social services that had previously partially played that role. A greater part of the burden was then dumped on individual families, primarily on women. Thatcher was trying to return to the conditions of Victorian capitalism when no welfare state existed. Today, women, largely as a result of their increased role in the workplace, are in a far stronger position than in the Victorian era. At the same time, the Tories and now New Labour have cut the welfare state to the bone leaving an increasing burden on working-class people, especially women.

It would be naive to suggest that a socialist government could just sweep aside sexism or racism and other prejudices, all deeply ingrained in this society. However, it could very quickly take economic measures – such as decent wages and jobs for all, free high-quality childcare, free universal education, good housing, widely available inexpensive high-quality restaurants and other measures – which would enormously ease the situation.

Longer term, the change in economic relations, the abolition of class divisions and the construction of a society based on democratic involvement and co-operation would also change social relations. Society would move away from hierarchies and the oppression and abuse of one group by another. Human relations would be freed from all the muck of capitalism.

Of course, there would be a transitional period where the new society still had to deal with the problems it inherited from the old. Nonetheless, many problems could be overcome quite quickly on the basis of the massively increased resources a democratic planned economy would provide. In the longer term, the highest stage of socialism would mean the development of a society free from all the divisions and oppression created by class society.

That does not mean that a socialist society would be monolithic or without controversy. Discussion and debate would be on a far higher level. Passionate arguments would undoubtedly take place. But they would be between parties and groupings with a common starting point – the betterment of humanity as a whole. This would be incomparable with capitalist society where political debate is restricted to a few at the top who spend most of their time disguising, supporting and justifying the indecent wealth and power of a tiny minority. It is possible to imagine a debate in a socialist society – which could be about, for example, the best method of energy production to meet the needs of humanity and the environment (wind or solar power, nuclear fusion or some other) – which could increase the understanding of the whole of society and lead to the best way forward being hammered out.

Capitalists' brutal record

The capitalists try to argue that a socialist government could only come to power by force. This is a red herring. It is they who have the most brutal record of violence imaginable, stopping at nothing to overturn democratic elections if they threaten the rule of capital. Thatcher has openly stated that she believes that General Pinochet's bloody coup in Chile in 1973, with the murder of tens of thousands of innocent people, was justified because of the threat of 'communism'.

Time and time again the capitalists have been prepared to use violence to protect their rule. Nevertheless, this resistance could be nullified by mobilising the mass of working-class people in support of a socialist government. The working class is potentially by far the most powerful force in society. If a socialist government mobilised that power in support of its policies an entirely peaceful transformation of society might be achievable. However, we are realistic. The ruling class will be prepared to use whatever means at its disposal to maintain its power and privileges. A socialist government could only defend itself if it mobilised the active support of the working class. And it would only be by demonstrating its power in practise that the working class could successfully defend its democratically elected socialist government.

If a socialist government were successfully established in Britain, would it come under attack from the rest of the capitalist world, in particular the US? There is no doubt that the ruling class of the US, the world's only superpower, would feel threatened by a socialist government and, if it thought it could get away with it, would use its overwhelming military might to try and crush a workers' state.

The ruling classes internationally are prepared to use any means to hold on to power. In a rare moment of straight talking one US strategic planner blurted out the real attitude of US imperialism in 1948: "We have 50% of the world's wealth but only 6.3% of its population. In this situation, our real job in the coming period... is to maintain this position of disparity. To do so, we have to dispense with all sentimen-

US imperialism in practice - vietnam

tality... we should cease thinking about human rights, the raising of living standards and democratisation."[25]

In a more recent moment of clarity, Thomas Friedman of the New York Times accurately declared: "The hidden hand of the market will never work without the hidden fist. McDonald's cannot flourish without McDonnell Douglas, the designer of the F-15. And the hidden fist that keeps the world safe for Silicon Valley's technologies is called the US Army, Air Force, Navy and Marine Corps."[26]

What could be clearer? The priority of the US Army is not the protection of democracy, of the weak and the innocent; it is the protection of US imperialism's profits by any means necessary. Nonetheless, it would be wrong to conclude that we are powerless before the 'hidden fist' of US imperialism.

It is true that the US ruling class was able to successfully use the horrific events of September 11 to temporarily win the support of the majority of US workers for the war on Afghanistan. (Far from being a war on terrorism, it has, in reality, meant the death of tens of thousands of innocent Afghanis and has done nothing to bring genuine democracy to the war ravaged country.)

However, it is one thing for imperialism to win support for taking action against the reactionary, anti-democratic Taliban regime. It would be an entirely different question to justify an attack on a popular socialist government which was making open appeals to the US working class for support. After all, the US's defeat in

Vietnam in the 1970s was a result of a combination of two factors – the movement in South Vietnam and the growing opposition to the war amongst the US working class. And the peasant-based, guerrilla struggle in South Vietnam had far less immediate resonance with workers in the US than a socialist government in an industrialised country would have.

The power of imperialism is potentially more limited today than it was almost a century ago when the Russian revolution took place in October 1917. Russia was a poor country, devastated by war and facing attack from 21 capitalist armies desperate to crush the newly-born Soviet Union.

Yet the Soviet Red Army, poorly equipped, hungry and tired, was able to declare victory in a little under three years. Why? Primarily, because of the working-class support internationally. Inspired by Russia, Europe was plunged into a series of revolutionary movements. A strike by Hungarian munitions workers in January 1918 spread like wildfire to Vienna, Berlin and throughout Germany, involving over two million workers. Their central demand was peace. In Finland an independent workers' republic was proclaimed. After months of fighting it was crushed with the help of German troops. Then on 4 November 1918 mutiny broke out at the German naval base of Kiel, igniting the German revolution. Within days every major city was in the hands of workers' councils. Mass strikes and a naval mutiny swept France. British soldiers mutinied, and the red flag was hoisted over the Clyde in Scotland. Strikes involving four million workers convulsed the USA in 1919.

These events, hardly mentioned in official history books, are a graphic illustration of how a workers' revolution will always have an incalculable effect internationally, provoking howls of outrage from big business and, at the same time, inspiring working-class people to come to its defence and follow its example.

On the battlefields, the Red Army were dropping thousands of leaflets appealing to the enemy troops. British and American soldiers began to mutiny. On the Black Sea, French sailors flew the red flag. The imperialists were compelled to withdraw their forces. For genuine socialism to have developed as a result of 1917 it would have been necessary for working-class people to have taken power in other countries. The potential for this existed – revolutionary movements took place in Germany, Hungary and other countries – but, tragically, they were defeated.

Today any genuine socialist government would face the same task, that of spreading the revolution internationally. However, the problems which imperialism faced in 1917 would be magnified 100 times today. The main reason for the governments of Britain, Germany, France, the US and other countries abandoning their assault on the Soviet Union was a fear that their armies and populations were being infected by the 'socialist plague'. With modern communications it would be far harder for the US or other capitalist governments to justify to their own populations taking action against a democratically elected socialist government.

Is there an easier way to change the world ?

Is socialism obsolete? Is there a new '21st century alternative' to capitalism that is 'more practicable' than socialism? Is it possible to reform capitalism? These are important questions. There is no point in making life harder than is necessary. If it were possible for some form of capitalism to take society forward and to improve the living conditions of humanity, socialism would remain nothing more than a dream. Instead, it is the very nature of capitalism which will lead to socialism becoming an idea which catches the imagination of millions.

Over the last decade increasing numbers of young people have declared themselves to be 'anti-capitalist'. This is an important step forward: it represents a new generation deciding to fight to change society. The anti-capitalist movement has a strong conviction that the existing order of things is unjust. However, there is

anti-capitalist demonstrators make their point in the the heart of british capitalism
- the city of london

no similarly clear conviction about what the alternative to capitalism should be. In general, the anti-capitalist movement has, as yet, only a vague idea of what it is fighting for, as opposed to what it is fighting against.

Nonetheless, there are a number of common themes that are being taken up by prominent representatives of the anti-capitalist movement. These include:

1. Belief in small-scale and individual action

For example, that co-operatives and non-profit making production can provide an alternative. Support for 'lifestyle' politics and the idea that it is possible to create an alternative society in the here-and-now, if only for a minority, with the aim of inspiring widespread emulation.

2. Hostility to party politics of any kind

The rejection of, or extreme scepticism towards, structured organisations, sometimes including those of the workers' movement, like trade unions, in favour of spontaneous individual action. This can include a rejection of the possibility of the working class being a major agent of social change.

3. Belief that new technology, particularly the internet, has fundamentally transformed the nature of struggle.

4. Scepticism about socialism

A belief that socialism would inevitably end in bureaucratic dictatorship as in the Soviet Union.

5. Scepticism towards all ideologies

A belief that the struggle to change society is best served by a mix-and-match approach, taking different ideas from many different ideologies.

6. Amongst some, particularly in the leadership of the movement, a belief that it is possible to reform capitalism into a more just system.

This is by no means an exhaustive list of the dominant ideas. Of course, many anti-capitalists do not support any of these ideas, and others only support some. Some people have already decided to adopt socialist ideas and reject many of the concepts listed above. However, these ideas are strong currents within anti-capitalism and form the main strands of the non-socialist arguments in the movement.

That is not to suggest that everything listed above is totally invalid. Who can argue against scepticism towards the mainstream political parties given their record? Who could dispute that some of the ideas on alternative education, child rearing, or health would represent a step forward if they could be widely applied? Nonetheless, these ideas do not provide a programme for an alternative society or, precisely, how capitalism can be overthrown and the possibility of building an alternative society realised. What is more, if these ideas are not superseded by a more worked-out programme they will have a damaging and limiting effect on the anti-capitalist movement in the next few years.

Islands of socialism?

The idea that it is possible to create alternative societies - 'islands of socialism' – within capitalism, is not new. Its most successful advocates were the utopian socialists, in particular Robert Owen, back in the early 19th century. Owen directed a cotton spinning mill at New Lanark, Scotland. He invented the infant school, with every child in the New Lanark colony attending from the age of two when in other cotton mills tiny children were being put to work. Whilst his competitors made their workers toil for 13 to 14 hours a day, in New Lanark the working day was ten-and-a-half hours. When a crisis in cotton stopped work for four months, his unemployed workers received their full wages all the time. And Owen went further, setting up a number of 'communist colonies' which were organised on a co-operative basis.

Owen was a pioneer to whom the socialist movement owes a debt. His ideas, developed 200 years ago, were far more advanced than those of Tony Blair today. However, Owen and other utopian socialists made a mistake in imagining that capitalism could be defeated simply by demonstrating the superiority of socialism in practise on a local and partial level. At the time Owen was working, capitalism was still in a relatively early stage of development – large scale industry was just beginning. The idea that the ruling class could be convinced to change by setting a good example seemed more reasonable than it does now.

Today the combined sales of the world's richest 200 companies are greater than the combined GDP of all but ten nations on earth.[27] In other words, overweening power is concentrated in a tiny number of hands whose priority is defending their own interests. It is clearly unviable to imagine that their resistance to fundamental change could be overcome merely by the good example of local co-operatives and communes. There is no alternative but to disempower the capitalist class by removing its control of the economy and the state.

Some argue that co-operatives, run on a 'fair' and 'equitable' basis, could gradually prove themselves to be more efficient than capitalist firms and that, therefore, they could come to dominate the economy. Unfortunately, there is overwhelming evidence that this is no more than wishful thinking. Understandably, when faced with the closure of a workplace, groups of workers sometimes resort to establishing workers' co-operatives to avoid redundancy. Far from representing a means of changing society, however, these co-operatives are subject to the laws of the capitalist society they exist in. This usually means that they fail because they cannot compete with 'unfair' capitalist companies, or capitalist relations resurface with increasing tensions between the workforce and the new management.

Does that mean that is impossible to escape and create an alternative lifestyle within capitalism? To some degree it is possible, but only for a small minority and only to a very limited extent. Small groups can do so, but it does not offer a solution for the mass of the population. In Britain for example, New Age travellers have succeeded on a small scale. Of course, people should have every right to choose this lifestyle without the harassment and violence they suffer at the hands of the police and the courts. But it is not really possible to escape the reality of capitalism. For example, capitalism will continue destroying the planet as long as it exists. If, as is possible, a nuclear exchange was to take place between India and Pakistan, nobody – no matter what their lifestyle – could escape the consequences.

In addition, only a tiny minority of people can, or want to, do without the 'normal' conveniences of life. For most people an alternative lifestyle of this kind is not a possibility. In today's society to give up work means to live in grinding poverty. Similarly, it is not realistic to expect the majority of people to give up 'consumer goods'. Modern capitalism encourages people to buy ever more unnecessary products. Nonetheless, many consumer goods genuinely improve the lives of working-class people. Fridges, central heating, washing machines, CD players and televisions, all improve peoples' lives. They are part of the accumulated standard of living of sections of the working class, won through the struggles of previous decades. However, on a world scale capitalism denies even the basic elements of civilisation to millions. We are fighting for a society where everyone has the right to a civilised life. Any movement based on the idea of people giving up the commodities they have won would be wrong – and would never win mass support!

It is true that many of these commodities, as they are produced and used under capitalism, play a role in destroying the environment. But this need not be the case. Modern technology could be used rationally and in an ecologically sustainable way. Surely we can keep washing machines without having environmentally destructive detergent? But this cannot be achieved by building an 'alternative society' on the margins of capitalism. It can only be achieved by changing the way that the whole of society operates.

The role of the working class

The low level of mass working-class action in the last decade has led to a tendency to look to other social forces and means of struggle for solutions. The idea of direct action by smaller groups of individuals (often as part of a wider movement) has taken hold of the imagination of many young people. Direct action of this kind has a very useful role to play. For example, the demonstrations and blockades in Seattle in 1999 showed how effective direct action can be. Long before the term was coined, direct action has been used in many struggles: from the suffragette movement for women's rights to the battle against the poll tax. However, it is only successful when it is an adjunct to, and not a replacement for, other forms of struggle.

Anti-capitalism has been effective because it has found a popular echo with millions of people around the world. When deciding if direct action by small groups will be effective or not we must always assess whether it will increase support among the mass of the working class and oppressed, or undermine it? Direct action is useful if it helps to build a mass movement. If it does not, it isn't.

Direct action is not a replacement for movements of the working class. The role of the workers in production gives it enormous power. The strength of the 'bulldozer revolution' in Serbia in 2000 (which overthrew Slobodan Milosevic) came primarily from the action of the working class. The miners who went on strike produced the raw material for two thirds of Serbia's energy. The recent 24-hour general strikes in Spain and Italy show graphically how the working class has the power to bring society to a halt. This makes the working class the most crucial force in the struggle to change society. Direct action can assist but in no way replace it. The working class is downtrodden by capitalism and the system strives to keep it ignorant and culturally backward. Yet it has an organised power and social cohesion like no other subject class. Of course, as the example of Serbia shows, without a clear political alternative the working class will not succeed in changing society. Nonetheless, it is potentially by far the most powerful force for social change.

Under capitalism the working class is compelled to struggle collectively through strikes, demonstrations and workplace occupations in order to win concessions and defend its interests. The decisive role of the working class in the socialist revolution arises because of the collective consciousness which it develops in the workplace as a result of its role in production, and because it faces common attacks from big business which it can only defeat through collective action. This allows it to prepare the basis for the collective, democratic control and management of society. And this lays the basis for establishing workers' democracy and beginning the task of building socialism. It is crucial that, in the struggle for socialism, the working class takes up the demands of all the exploited and oppressed layers in society. But because of its relation to the means of production, it is the working class that plays the decisive role in changing society.

Does this apply in Britain today?

Are working-class people apathetic? Do we have to rely on others to lead the struggle? Surely, some argue, revolutionary movements have only taken place in so-called 'third world' countries. And, where they have taken place in the West, it was in the long-gone, dim-and-hazy past. These arguments, commonplace today, are not new. For example, they were widely expounded by left-wing groups in Europe weeks before May 1968. Then, as if from nowhere, the greatest general strike in history erupted in France. This demonstrated how dangerous it is for socialists to take a superficial view of society!

France in 1968 was in no way an economically backward country. Real incomes were rising by an average of 5% a year. In ten years car ownership had doubled, as had the number of washing machines in private homes. Purchases of fridges had trebled. Over one million second homes had been bought. Television ownership was up five-fold.

At the same time, work was intensifying: hours had increased substantially to an average of 45 a week. Unemployment had risen by 70% since 1960. The regime in the factories was extremely repressive, with private armies of armed thugs policing the production lines. The government of Charles de Gaulle mixed parliamentarism with autocratic, authoritarian methods of control.

The movement was begun by students who were viciously attacked by the CRS paramilitary police. Then workers began to mobilise as well. The demonstrations were phenomenal - a million marched in Paris with hundreds of thousands more protesting throughout France. By 21 May, ten million people were taking part in a general strike

France 1968 was not an isolated incident. There were many similar revolutionary movements in the 1960s and 1970s, such as Chile (1973) and Portugal (1974). Today the working class worldwide is, in terms of numbers, cohesion and social weight as potentially strong as in the 1960s and 1970s. However, its understanding is not as great. The collapse of the Stalinist regimes and the wave of capitalist triumphalism that followed have led to a relative pushing back of the consciousness of the working class. Socialism is not yet seen as a viable alternative to capitalism to the degree that it was in the past. Nonetheless, when the working class lifts its little finger the world shakes and tyrants are overthrown. The mighty movement led by the Serbian miners brushed Milosevic aside. In Argentina, four presidents, all trying to continue neo-liberal attacks on the impoverished working and middle classes, were forced from office within two weeks as the oppressed masses arose.

chile 1973 - US backed military coup

In Britain (see Chapter Three), in addition to the international factors, there are also specific national reasons for the undermining of confidence in the strength of the workers' movement. In the 1970s the British working class was one of the most combative in Europe. However, the defeats inflicted by Thatcherism resulted in the driving down of living conditions in relative and absolute terms for sections of the British working class.

Sometimes defeats can lead to a temporary lack of confidence or stunning of the movement. To a degree, this is what has happened. Nonetheless, it would be impressionistic to believe that this is permanent or fail to see the opposite side of the process. Alongside this lack of confidence there is a seething anger against the existing order. At a certain stage, this will explode into mighty struggles that will demonstrate once again the power of the British working class.

Some argue that the changes that have taken place in the structure of industry have fatally undermined the strength of the working class. It is true that more people are employed in smaller workplaces than was the case 20 years ago. This can potentially undermine the feeling of collective strength and make organising effectively more difficult. However, half of Britain's workers still work in workplaces of 200 or more, with 30% in workplaces of 500 or more, compared to only 17% who work in workplaces with 29-50 employees.[28]

It is also true that more workers are employed in casual, non-union work than was the case 20 years ago. Yet it would be wrong to conclude that this fundamentally undermines the workers' potential strength. When the general trade unions were first formed in the late 19th and early 20th centuries workers had to overcome phenomenal obstacles. Casual work, in its most brutal form, was the norm. Dockers, for example, had to line up on the docks in cages every morning waiting to see if the foreman would pick them for work that day. After mighty battles they went on to become one of the most highly-organised groups of workers in Britain. Today the working class has not been driven back that far, but organising and fighting for the rights of agency and casual workers, and those employed in small, non-union sweatshops, will form part of the rebuilding of the workers' movement.

Does the internet change any of this?

Socialists should use every available way of spreading our ideas. The internet is one such means and it is extremely useful, dramatically increasing the speed with which information can be transmitted. But it is only a tool in the hands of living forces which are not made up of computers but people.

Big business uses the internet for its own ends. We have to use it for ours - that is, to build a movement of the working class and oppressed to overthrow capitalism. It will be the movement's strength on the ground, not in cyberspace, that will determine its success or failure. In the mass protests in the Philippines in 2001, for example, demonstrations were built for using text messaging on mobile phones. But president Joseph Estrada would not have been overthrown if text messaging was all that people had done, it was necessary to physically participate.

What's more, under capitalism there are definite limits to the degree that we can use information technology. The majority of the world's population still have to walk more than two miles to reach a telephone. They do not have electricity. They certainly don't have access to the internet! Even in Britain, only a minority of working-class families are on-line. Everyone who uses the internet relies on service providers, such as Virgin or AOL, the vast majority of which are owned by multimillionaires. There is no doubt that, if they considered that the capitalist system was threatened, these people would be prepared to sabotage protests organised through their companies.

Do we need to be organised?

Understandably, given the record of the Stalinist dictatorships, as well as the example set by the right-wing trade union and labour movement leaders, there is an extreme scepticism about organisations amongst many young activists. A fear exists that any organisation will lead to bureaucracy. In reality, organisation is a vital prerequisite for democracy. It is a myth that any demonstration takes place entirely spontaneously. Every event is organised to some degree. For all the anti-capitalist protests, for example, people wrote and printed leaflets, updated the websites and so on. However, without organisation and democratic structures, there is no way to take part in collective decision making. 'Self-organisation', far from preventing the development of leaders, as its advocates claim, simply means that the people taking the decisions - regardless of whether those decisions are good or bad - are not accountable to the movement.

Self-organisation is also very limited from a purely practical point of view. Collective decision making - where a debate takes place, a vote is taken and a majority decision reached, which is then abided to by all - is a basic prerequisite for effective action. It is clearly crucial, for example, if a strike is to be successful.

Naomi Klein, an enthusiastic supporter of self-organisation, has herself pointed out some of its practical limitations. She described an incident during the anti-World Bank protests in Washington DC. The demonstrators had surrounded the headquarters of the World Bank and IMF and had blocked every exit. The demonstrators had to decide whether to stop the blocking the exits and march on to the main demonstration or to continue their blockade. Klein explains: "The

International Socialist Resistance - anti-capitalist demonstrators in brussels

compromise the council came up with was telling. 'OK, everybody listen up,' Kevin Danaher shouted into a megaphone. 'Every intersection has autonomy. If the intersection wants to stay locked down, that's cool. If it wants to come to the Ellipse [the main demonstration], that's cool too.' This was impeccably fair and democratic, but there was just one problem - it made absolutely no sense. Sealing off the access points had been a co-ordinated action. If some intersections now opened up and other, rebel camp intersections stayed occupied, delegates on their way out of the [World Bank] meeting could just hang a right instead of a left, and they would be home free. Which, of course, is precisely what happened.

"As I watched clusters of protestors get up and wander off while others stayed seated, defiantly guarding, well, nothing, it struck me as an apt metaphor for the strengths and weaknesses of the nascent activist network."[29]

This is a graphic illustration of why collective decision making is vital. Such a situation, as well as making the blockade completely ineffective, could have left the remaining blockaders vulnerable to attack from the police.

It is not only for individual demonstrations that collective organisation is needed. The might of capitalism cannot be defeated on the basis of spontaneity alone. Individual movements can and do take place 'spontaneously', without any formal organisation. But they are far more effective when they are organised. For example, anger against the iniquitous poll tax was not created by any campaign but by the tax itself. However, the poll tax was defeated by an organised campaign of mass non-payment (led by the Anti-Poll Tax Federation in which Militant played a leading role). Without tens of thousands being actively organised in the anti-poll tax unions set up throughout Britain the poll tax would not have been defeated.

Revolutionary movements also take place spontaneously. But capitalism is an enormously powerful system and the working class, while it has numbers on its side, is divided into many different layers and sections. Capitalism cannot be successfully and permanently removed without a workers' organisation which unites these different layers and has the necessary determination, experience and roots in the working class.

As Leon Trotsky explained in The History of the Russian Revolution: "They [parties and leaders] constitute not an independent, but nevertheless a very important element in the process. Without a guiding organisation the energy of the masses would dissipate like steam not enclosed in a piston-box. But nevertheless what moves things is not the piston or the box, but the steam."

In other words, it is the masses who change society, but organisation in the form of a party is an essential tool without which they cannot succeed in defeating the capitalists.

Many in the anti-capitalist movement believe that any attempt to build a Marxist party is doomed to end in bureaucracy and failure. They see all parties as attempting to impose their own set of ideas on others. Of course, it is correct to reject 'dogmatic Marxism', which sees in every movement a mere repetition of the past. Klein, when asked if her book, No Logo, is a manifesto for the anti-capitalist movement, said: "There is no Das Kapital for the anti-corporate movement. One of the best things about this movement is that no one is handing down a manifesto from on high."[30]

She goes on to explain that she sees the eclectic ideological nature of the anti-capitalist movement as a strength. Klein describes it as "taking a little bit from Marxism, a little bit from socialism, from environmentalism, from anarchism, and also a lot of inspiration from even older places and more indigenous theories about self-determination".[31]

We share some of the approaches of Klein. No Logo imaginatively connects with the new generation that is drawing anti-capitalist conclusions. However, the problem with her approach is that it ignores the fact that some ideas are more effective in aiding struggle than others. When trade unionists debate which way forward for their strike, the strategy they adopt matters. It can make the difference between victory and defeat. This is also true on a broader scale. To give just one example: as previously mentioned, in 1973 Salvador Allende, the democratically elected socialist president of Chile, was overthrown by General Pinochet's bloody CIA-backed coup. Allende and tens of thousands of others were killed. In the run up to the coup Allende made a number of mistaken decisions, including trying to pacify the generals by bringing Pinochet into the cabinet. As Marxists argued at the time, had he taken different decisions, the tragic outcome could have been prevented.

One of the roles of a party should be to act as a memory bank of the working class and the oppressed. History, as the saying goes, belongs to the victor. Too true. And while we live in a capitalist society it will be the history that suits capitalism that will dominate. It is therefore necessary for a working-class party to independently remember previous struggles from a working-class standpoint - both defeats and victories - in order to apply the lessons of those struggles to the situation today. If we do not do this and fail to draw the appropriate conclusions - for example, the need to be organised or the role of the working class - we are condemning every new generation to start from scratch and to relearn, through bitter defeats, the mistakes of the past.

History is a moving picture. It does not repeat itself exactly but this does not mean that the past is irrelevant. Many activists believe that the fall of the Stalinist regimes has changed the world so completely that all the struggles before 1990 are now irrelevant. This is a huge exaggeration. The collapse of Stalinism was an ideological victory for big business and has had a major effect on the consciousness and outlook of the working class. However, it has not in any way changed the fundamental nature of capitalism or class society. Our enemy is same enemy our forebears fought. We can still learn from both the victories and the tragic defeats that they suffered in their struggle to overthrow capitalism.

By applying the method of Marxism to analyse the world and draw up a programme to change it, it is possible for a party to make the difference between the success or failure of mass movements.

Nonetheless, any Marxist party worthy of the name does not 'hand down a manifesto from on high' but has a living, dynamic relationship with the struggles that are taking place - aiding them but also learning from them. This was true in the past. The Bolshevik party, which led the Russian revolution, did not invent the idea of soviets (workers' committees). In fact, soviets first appeared during an earlier revolution in 1905. However, it was Trotsky, Lenin and the Bolsheviks who understood their significance and went on to raise the demand 'all power to the Soviets' in 1917. Without the lead given by the Bolshevik party, the Russian revolution would not have taken place.

Doesn't the Russian experience prove that a party leads to bureaucracy?

But didn't subsequent developments in Russia expose a fundamental link between the Bolshevik party and Stalinism? And does that mean that any attempt to replace capitalism will end in dictatorship? It is not surprising that these doubts are widespread. The ruling class has milked the collapse of the Soviet Union for everything it is worth in order to bolster its own system. This is reflected throughout society. Owning and controlling much of the planet, the capitalists have enormous power to influence ideas. In the universities, post-modernism – which is just scepticism dressed up as a new philosophy - is the flavour of the month. It is fashionable to believe that it is naive or dangerous to dare to try and change anything. Of course, this suits big business which does not want anything to change. But for the rest of us, fashionable 'detachment' means accepting that we are powerless.

Capitalism has only existed for something over 300 years. On the scale of human history that is nothing, a tiny speck of time. It is true that during that time capitalism has transformed the planet - bringing incredible technology alongside devastating want - yet it is no more permanent than any other means by which human society has been organised.

Despite the fact that the Soviet Union collapsed, writers still churn out books by the truckload, attempting to show the 'irrelevance' of the Russian revolution. This first successful attempt to overthrow capitalism still evokes enormous fear for big business. We should not despair at its failure. We should, rather, learn the lessons from what went wrong. To do so it is necessary to look back at the revolution itself and the years that followed.

Russia 1917 was the first time that capitalism was overthrown by working-class people. The revolution was led by the Bolshevik party. However, it was organised through the soviets – elected councils of workers, soldiers and peasants. The basic demands of the Bolsheviks were for 'bread, peace and land', but they explained that only by breaking with capitalism were these demands achievable. The Bolsheviks won the leadership of the working class of Russia, not by force but by patiently explaining their ideas within the soviets. Alongside the leadership of the Bolsheviks the Russian working class was able to come to power. How did this wonderful movement - in which millions of downtrodden people were genuinely empowered because they took power in their own hands – end up in what the Soviet Union tragically became?

Marx had thought it most likely that capitalism would be defeated first in the most economically developed countries. It was here, after all, where the working class was at its most powerful and the industrial basis existed for the transition to socialism. Instead, in October 1917, the chain of world capitalism broke at its weakest link. The Soviet government inherited an underdeveloped society in a state of disintegration, exhausted by three years of world war. This made the building of

images of the original leaders of the russian revolution - and their fate

socialism far harder than it would have been in a more economically advanced country. The task of spreading the revolution internationally, therefore, took on a burning urgency.

The pressures on the Soviet Union

Within Russia the old ruling class fought against the revolution with every means at its disposal. The imperialist powers intervened directly, funding and arming the counter-revolutionary forces, known as the 'Whites'. From May 1918 to the spring of 1921 civil war raged.

Alongside the determination of the workers and peasants in the Soviet Union, international solidarity was decisive in the victory of the Red Army. However, while they managed to help defeat the counter-revolution in Russia, the revolutionary movements in other countries did not succeed in taking power. The leadership of the Bolsheviks understood that this meant that their victory would be temporary. Lenin, the leader of the Bolshevik party, explained: "In all our agitation... we must explain that the misfortune which has fallen upon us is an international misfortune, that there is no way out of it but the international revolution."[32]

Why were the revolutionary movements in other countries, such as Germany, defeated in the aftermath of the Russian revolution? After all, the working class was far stronger in Germany and they had witnessed the success in Russia. The biggest difference was the lack of a Bolshevik-type party. The Bolsheviks had, over a long period of time, become rooted in the working class. Unlike any other party in Russia it had not buckled under the immense pressure to capitulate to right-wing reaction - despite the vacillation of a number of its leaders. Under the leadership of Lenin, the Bolsheviks were prepared to lead the working class to power.

In no other country did a party with a similar authority or outlook exist. The only international socialist organisation, the Second International of which the Bolsheviks had been a part, had shattered at the beginning of the first world war. The parties of the Second International had become powerful in the early years of the 20th century. However, their leaders, while claiming to be Marxists, had become privileged and remote from the workers' struggle. Their political degeneration was completed when they, almost to a man and woman, supported the interests of 'their own' imperialist, national, capitalist class in the first world war at the beginning in 1914.

This meant that the Bolsheviks had no international party to organise support for the Russian revolution. They immediately set about trying to create one. The Communist International was founded in March 1919. But it was made up of many disparate and inexperienced elements. In Germany the most experienced revolutionaries, the heroic figures of Karl Liebknecht and Rosa Luxemburg, were murdered in the counter-revolution in January 1919. The younger generation that flocked to the Communist International did not have the experience or authority to build the mass revolutionary parties that could lead the working class in their respective countries to power. Although there were many opportunities for the working class to take power, particularly in Germany, those opportunities were missed. Surely, the lesson to draw from this is not that it is impossible to win socialism, but that an international party with the kind of strengths that the Bolshevik party had in Russia is necessary.

The Russian revolution was left isolated. And this was the principal cause of its degeneration. Lenin, just before the Russian revolution, had laid out four safeguards to protect a fledgling workers' state from the rise of a privileged bureaucratic elite. They were:

1. Free and democratic elections with the right of recall of all officials.
2. No official to receive a higher wage than a skilled worker.
3. No standing army or police force, but the armed people.
4. Gradually, for all administrative tasks to be done in turn by all: "Every cook should be prime minister," "when everyone is a 'bureaucrat' in turn, nobody can be a bureaucrat".

If implemented, these guidelines would have protected Russia from degeneration. But it was impossible, despite the efforts of the revolutionaries, to fully implement them in such an isolated and impoverished country. Economic backwardness has a devastating effect, causing food shortages and a lack of basic necessities. Trotsky compared the development of a bureaucracy to a policeman controlling a queue: "When there are enough goods in a store, the purchasers can come when they want to. When there are few goods, the purchasers are compelled to stand in line. When the lines are very long, it is necessary to appoint a policeman to keep order. Such is the starting point for the Soviet bureaucracy. It 'knows' who is to get something and who has to wait."[33]

In this situation it was inevitable that a bureaucratic caste would develop and take control. Joseph Stalin was a hideous dictator but he did not create the bureaucracy, rather he was a living expression of it. It is true that Stalin was an 'Old Bolshevik' (a member of the party from before the revolution) but it is absolutely false to say that Stalinism arose inevitably from the nature of the Bolshevik party. Every capitalist historian who asserts this is forced to ignore one incontrovertible fact: that to consolidate his power Stalin had to have his former comrades murdered. Lenin died in 1924 and could therefore be turned into an icon – his image used in the interests of the bureaucracy. His words were distorted beyond any recognition to back up Stalin. In fact, Lenin had tried to warn against Stalin in the last testament that he wrote shortly before he died. Practically every member of the Central Committee of the Bolshevik party in 1917 was dead by 1940, most of them murdered on Stalin's orders. As a consequence of brutal purges it is estimated that Stalin's murderous toll in the 1930s totalled between 12-15 million people.

Nonetheless, the voice of genuine socialism did not give up without a fight. The Left Opposition, led by Trotsky, fought back. Leopold Trepper, who led the Soviet spy ring in Nazi Germany, said of the Trotskyists: "All those who did not rise up against the Stalinist machine are responsible, collectively responsible. I am no exception to this verdict. But who did protest at the time? Who rose up to voice his outrage?

"The Trotskyites can lay claim to this honour. Following the example of their leader, who was rewarded for his obstinacy with the end of an ice-axe, they fought Stalinism to the death, and they were the only ones who did. By the time of the great purges they could only shout their rebellion in the freezing wastelands where they had been dragged in order to be exterminated. In the camps, their conduct was admirable. But their voices were lost in the tundra.

"Today, the Trotskyites have a right to accuse those who once howled along with the wolves. Let them not forget, however, that they had the enormous advantage over us of having a coherent political system capable of replacing Stalinism. They had something to cling to in the midst of their profound distress at seeing the revolution betrayed. They did not 'confess' for they knew that their confession would serve neither the party nor socialism."[34]

Heroism, however, was not, in itself, enough. The only way the Left Opposition could win was by a successful revolution in another country. Without such a revolution the Soviet Union was left isolated. A privileged layer rose to the top and elbowed aside the working class and abandoned the revolution's internationalist perspective. This led to the utterly false idea of socialism in one country. Initially, the mistakes of the growing bureaucracy contributed to the defeat of the German working class. Then, as faith in international revolution dimmed further, the reformist tendencies of the bureaucracy were reinforced. In Spain in the 1930s, where the working class had power within its grasp, the Stalinists consciously derailed the revolution, allowing the murder of the best fighters for socialism.

In 1940 Trotsky was murdered in Mexico on the orders of Stalin. Stalin's purges were not simply 'evil', they were designed to put a river of blood between the revolution of 1917 and the reality of Stalinism.

Today capitalist historians are most eager to bury the true history of 1917 under a pile of slander. It is the job of socialists to look more closely and discover the real story, the lessons of which can help guide our struggles today. This firstly means refuting the calumny that there is an inevitable link between organising to change society and the development of a Stalinist bureaucracy. The Bolshevik party was very democratic and its methods bore absolutely no resemblance to the methods of Stalinism. Of course, it was not some kind of ahistorical, perfect model and it would be foolish to imagine that such a thing could exist. The Bolsheviks had some weaknesses but they also had many strengths. These strengths are what make the Bolsheviks stand on a higher level than any other party that has yet existed, enabling them to lead the working class to power and to overthrow the capitalist order.

The world has changed dramatically over the last century. We have much to learn from the Bolsheviks. However, the oppressive tsarist regime meant that the Bolsheviks had to work in underground conditions and use clandestine methods. Today in Britain we work in a capitalist democracy which, at the moment at least, allows us to organise relatively freely. We are able to be very open, to emphasise democracy and the vital necessity of listening to, and learning from, the working class.

Can capitalism be reformed or controlled?

Although it is rarely articulated, a section of the anti-capitalist movement, particularly some of the leading figures, does not aim to overthrow capitalism but to reform it. In Britain, two of the most popular books by leading anti-capitalists have been Naomi Klein's No Logo and George Monbiot's Captive State - the Corporate Takeover of Britain. Both give searing accounts of the reality of globalised capitalism and, in particular, the power of the multinationals. Fundamentally, however, their conclusions amount to the idea that it is possible to exert control over these same multinationals and to tip the balance away from big business and towards the oppressed.

Klein, for example, concludes her book by calling for citizens "through unions, laws and international treaties" to "take control of their own labour conditions and of the ecological impact of industrialisation". She claims that this was achieved in the 1930s in the US and could be done again, this time on "a global scale".

Monbiot's conclusions are similar. He calls on mass movements to prevent "any faction - the corporations, the aristocracy, the armed forces, even, for that matter, trade unions and environment groups from wielding excessive power".

Both authors are correct to call for mass movements to challenge the power of the multinationals. They are also correct to say that working-class people and the oppressed could win victories and improve their living conditions as a result of such movements. Every improvement in working-class life - the welfare state, the right to vote, wage increases, even the right to ramble - has been won as a result of determined struggle.

Socialists should fully support many of the reforms argued for in the anti-capitalist movement. We support, for example, the cancellation of 'third world debt'. The neo-colonial world spends $13 on debt repayment for every $1 it receives in grants from the imperialist countries. For most countries concerned even paying the interest on this 'debt' is crippling. In sub-Saharan Africa governments spend more on servicing debt – $300 billion (£200 billion) – than on the health and education of children. These ever mounting debts are cynically used by the agencies of imperialism, the IMF and the World Bank, to pressure neo-colonial governments into toeing the line. Toeing the line involves privatisation, cuts in state spending and the opening up of the market to US and Western imperialism! But while we campaign for the cancellation of the debt, it would be wrong to argue that this measure alone would be enough. As long as power resides with a few predominantly US-owned corporations, whose interests are defended by US imperialism, it is clear that poverty will remain the norm for the bulk of humanity.

Similarly, we support the idea of campaigning for a tax on capital flows, for example, the Tobin Tax, a proposed tax on international financial transactions of around 0.5% which would be used to alleviate world poverty. Such a tax, if implemented, could raise enormous sums of money. Even the modest Tobin Tax might raise £140 billion a year! However, the 'if implemented' proviso is an important one. Who could implement the Tobin Tax? How would it be possible to separate the introduction of such a measure in a world of uncontrolled capital flows – which national governments are unable to control – from the need for wider, socialist measures? When the Labour government of 1964 introduced a mild corporation tax, the British ruling class went on a 'strike of capital'. Because that government remained within the framework of capitalism, it was compelled to retreat and water down the tax until it became completely harmless to capitalist interests. Without a state monopoly of foreign trade and the nationalisation of the banks, a Tobin Tax could not work. It would be like sneaking up on a wild tiger and trying to surreptitiously pull its teeth out one by one.

This does not preclude the ruling class of different countries, even advanced capitalist countries, from introducing taxes on capital movements on a national basis in the future. At the moment, the imperialist powers would bitterly oppose such measures. Nonetheless, in order to bail out capitalism in an extreme economic crisis, they would be prepared to take all kinds of seemingly unthinkable steps. However, any such taxes would be limited to a national basis and, crucially, would not be used to alleviate world poverty. They would be implemented in the interests of the capitalists.

No matter how hard people fight, or how many progressive laws are passed, capitalism will never be a 'fair' system. As previously explained, capitalism is based on private property and the exploitation of working people's labour power. At every opportunity, the bosses will attack the living conditions of working people to increase their own profits. As Marx stated, while the capitalist class owns the means of production it will exploit the working class. When wealth and power are concentrated in an ever smaller group of multinational companies, the idea that they can

demonstrators against IMF and World Bank in nigeria

be controlled and made to act in a 'fair' way is more utopian than ever.

What is more, capitalism is a system in crisis. Klein and Monbiot put forward what are fundamentally Keynesian ideas - increasing government spending (traditionally on socially useful infrastructure projects and increasing welfare) to boost the economy. Klein harks back to the 1930s when US president Franklin D Roosevelt implemented the Keynesian New Deal.

However, it is wrong to imagine that Keynesian policies can solve the problems of capitalism. In the whole history of capitalism there was only a very short period when the living standards of a majority of workers in the advanced capitalist countries improved steadily – from 1950 to the mid-1970s. This post-war economic upswing has been the only period when capitalism appeared that it might partially overcome its problems. For particular historical reasons - including the massive destruction of capital in Europe and the deaths of 55 million people during the second world war - capitalism grew extremely rapidly and could therefore afford to make concessions to the working class. Average annual growth in the 'advanced capitalist countries' was, in real terms, 5% during the post-war upswing. By contrast, in the 1990s it averaged 2.3%.

After the war, Keynesian policies were very much in vogue and are often associated with this time. However, while they helped to prolong the upswing, they did not create it. In fact, when the economic upswing reached its limits in the early 1970s, Keynesian policies began to exacerbate all the problems in the system, leading to massive inflation.

Once the upswing had reached its limits, and came to an end in the early 1970s, big business has attempted to take back all that it had once conceded. This included a dramatic turn away from Keynesian policies. It is likely that in the future, under the impact of economic crises, the ruling class in some countries will be forced to reintroduce some of these methods again. To an extent this has already begun. After all, while the US government criticises other countries for carrying out Keynesian-type, protectionist measures, this is the only description that can be given to Bush's massive 'farm bill' subsidy increases given to US agri-business.

The fundamental weakness of capitalism means that these policies will fail to recreate the relative stability of the post-war upswing. Japan has already attempted to use neo-Keynesian methods to kick-start its economy, the second largest in the world, with no success. After a decade of stagnation Japanese capitalism has now slumped back into recession. Unemployment is the highest for over 50 years. The growing anger in Japanese society is so palpable that the ruling class is terrified. This has given rise to the latest joke amongst Japanese bankers: 'What is the difference between Japan and Argentina? Two years.'

Notwithstanding the improvements won during the two decades after the second world war, the whole history of the 20th century proves that it is not possible to 'reform' capitalism. Klein talks about the magnificent movements of the working class that took place in the 1930s. These movements and the catastrophic crisis of capitalism forced the Roosevelt government to introduce the New Deal. But this did not stabilise capitalism. The crisis of capitalism in the 1920s and 1930s led to the rise of fascism and the nightmare of the second world war. It was only after this orgy of destruction that capitalism was able to enjoy a brief period of stability and growth.

It is the grim reality of 21st century capitalism that will lead a new generation to rediscover the ideas of genuine socialism. In general, humanity never goes back to its starting point but takes on board the accumulated experiences of previous generations. The ideas of Marx, Engels, Lenin and Trotsky are already being searched out by a minority in the young anti-capitalist movement. In the future it will be working-class people in their millions who rediscover and adopt the ideas and methods of Marxism.

The Socialist Party

The Socialist Party is not just an organisation that argues the case for socialism. We use our Marxist analysis as a tool to attempt to guide struggles to defend and improve the living conditions of working-class people. Even in the 1960s, when we had very small forces, we played a crucial role in a number of battles, such as the 1964 apprentices' strike. In the 1980s and the early 1990s we led two of the most important mass struggles of the working class of the time, the battle of Liverpool City Council and the mass campaign against the poll tax. We were then called 'Militant' and were the major Marxist current within the Labour Party.

Militant supporters were expelled from the Labour Party by the right wing in the late 1980s and early 1990s. We explained that the expulsion of Militant supporters would be the thin end of the wedge and that a purging of socialist ideas would follow close behind. Unfortunately, we were proved correct as Blairism established a stranglehold on the Labour Party. It was not only socialists who were expelled along with socialist ideology, even the idea of defending the living standards of the

militant, the socialist party's forerunner campaigning against the poll-tax in scotland

working class was trashed.

While the New Labour leaders have almost entirely expunged class struggle from their party they cannot wipe it out of British society so easily. The major battles we led or participated in during the last 20 years will be dwarfed by the struggles of the next 20. But the victories we have so far been able to contribute to will be remembered and their lessons will be useful for the new generation.

From 1983-87 we played a leading role on Liverpool City Council as it fought against Tory government cuts. For having the temerity to stand up to Thatcher we were vilified by the Labour leaders. Yet, if every Labour council in the country had taken the same stand, not only would the Tory government have had to abandon its cuts packages, it would have been swept from office. Even though Liverpool City Council was isolated alongside Lambeth Council, under attack from all sides, it was able to secure a major victory. In 1984 it won a '95% victory' when it extracted an extra £60 million in funding from the government. This was not just a battle of the council but a struggle that engulfed the entire city with demonstrations of 50,000 and more. Millions of workers across the country supported the movement.

The·results of the Liverpool battle still stand in bricks and mortar. Some of the main achievements of the council were:

Housing: Fourteen inner-city and two other housing estates, with a population of over 40,000, were completely transformed. Five thousand council houses were built, all with front and back gardens and their own private entrance, 4,400 council houses and flats and 4,115 private-sector homes were renovated.

Education: Five hundred extra education staff were employed, six new nurseries opened and four colleges were built.

Leisure: Six new sports centres were constructed. Sports facilities were free for the unemployed, disabled people, those in receipt of a pension and school leavers.

Jobs: The council took on an extra 800 workers and 16,489 jobs were created by the house building programme.

In the early 1990s we played a leading role in the battle against the hated poll tax. Eighteen million people refused to pay it. On 31 March 1990, 50,000 marched in Glasgow, with over 200,000 in London. (The London demonstration ended in rioting after the police viciously attacked the march.) The mass movement against the poll tax was responsible not only for defeating the tax but also forced the resignation of its architect, the 'Iron Lady', Maggie Thatcher. These two examples are the biggest, but far from the only, mass struggles our party led in this period. For example, we also initiated school student strikes in 1985 which defeated the Tories plans to remove the right of 16- and 17-year-olds to claim unemployment benefit (this measure was unfortunately forced through four years later).

In 1992 we set up Youth Against Racism in Europe (YRE), which played a key role in the battle against the neo-Nazi British National Party (BNP). YRE's first act was to organise a demonstration in Brussels against the far-right of 40,000 young people from across Europe. In 1994 YRE co-organised a demonstration of 50,000 in Welling, South London, which succeeded in getting the BNP's headquarters closed down. When the BNP got a councillor elected on the Isle of Dogs, East London, YRE played a crucial role in marginalising the neo-fascists and assisting the Asian community in organising against the BNP. As a result of the anti-Nazi movement of the early 1990s the BNP were pushed backed into virtual non-existence. Now, as they are beginning to grow again, YRE is once more to the fore of the struggle to defeat them.

On coming to power, New Labour swiftly abolished the student grant and introduced student tuition fees. We responded by founding Save Free Education (SFE). Over the following years SFE has led a series of student strikes, protests and occupations alongside a non-payment campaign, and calls for a living grant and the abolition of the fees. The campaign continues. Fees have been abolished in Scotland (although the graduate tax system that has replaced them is far from progressive) and their days seem to be numbered in Wales as well. New Labour in England has floated the possibility of abolishing them, but seems to have retreated for now. It is because of the huge unpopularity of student fees that New Labour is on the retreat.

militant labour - campaigning against the bnp

But it is also due to the effect of the campaigns initiated by SFE, not least in popularising the idea of mass non-payment. When fees were first introduced, The Times Higher Education Supplement commented that "payment of tuition fees could become as voluntary as payment of the poll tax". (30 July 1999) Whilst non-payment is not taking place in the same organised way as during the anti-poll tax campaign, the major factor forcing New Labour to reconsider its policy is the scale of non-payment. It is estimated that around 30% of fees have gone unpaid and in the more working-class universities the figure is higher.

There are countless other campaigns that we have been involved in over the last decade – some more successful than others. There was the battle against the Criminal Justice Act in 1994, the 'no blood for oil' campaign against the Gulf war in 1990, and innumerable struggles against the privatisation of our public services. However, whilst we fight heart and soul in every campaign in which we are involved, we also understand the limited nature of even the greatest victories whilst we live in a capitalist society. That is why we always link day-to-day struggles with a socialist programme. It is only by a socialist transformation of society that the working class will be able to win decent living conditions and justice on a permanent basis.

Today

In the last decade there have not been national struggles of the working class on the scale of the 1980s and early 1990s. However, the first breezes of the coming storm in British society are beginning to stir. In all of them – the movement against war in Afghanistan, anti-capitalist May Day demonstrations, and increasing strike action - we have taken a full and active part. We have also helped organise hundreds of local struggles against the barrage of attacks on the working class. To give just one from hundreds of examples, in Sheffield we played a leading role in a successful campaign to close a toxic waste disposal plant in Killamarsh. The Press Officer of the campaign explained how he viewed our party: "[The Socialist Party] for the last two years stood side by side with us as we battled against this huge multinational... [They] showed us how to protest, how to sustain it over all the time of the campaign... Now our campaign has become a blueprint of what can be achieved by ordinary people against these big chemical companies."

Public representatives

As a result of our role in different campaigns we have been able to build real roots in communities. We are the only socialist organisation in England and Wales to have had public representatives elected, with Socialist Party councillors in Coventry and Lewisham, London. All of our public representatives take no more than the average wage of a skilled worker.

In the trade unions we are to the forefront in the battle to defend jobs and working conditions, and in overcoming the obstacle of the right-wing trade union leaders. In 2000 a member of our party, Roger Bannister, stood for the position of general secretary in UNISON (the biggest trade union in Britain) and won 71,021 votes (over 31%). We have eleven members on the National Executive Committees of six of the main trade unions.

The Socialist Party is part of the Committee for a Workers' International (CWI) which organises in 33 countries, on every inhabited continent of the globe. Many of the sections of the CWI have an established record of leading mass struggles, for example, in Nigeria, Sri Lanka, Sweden and Ireland. Our sister party in Ireland succeeded in getting Joe Higgins elected as a TD in the Irish parliament, the Dáil. We also have councillors in Ireland, Netherlands, Kazakhstan and Sweden. Compared to the scale of the task we have set ourselves the forces of the CWI are very small.

campaigning for free education

However, regardless of the size of our international groups, we have always started from an international standpoint. The need for a global organisation flows from the development of capitalism itself which has created a world market and a world working class. This idea is even more important today in the period of globalisation. The linking together of companies, continents and different national economies has taken place on a hitherto unimagined scale and adds urgency to the need for Marxists to organise internationally.

The importance of ideas

Our party's orientation and action are integrally linked to our ideas. Without an understanding of Marxism, and a capacity to develop and apply it to new situations, we would not have been able to play the role we have in several mass movements. That method has also enabled us to comprehend the changes in the world since the collapse of Stalinism. That is why our party, unlike most others left organisations, has been able to withstand the difficulties of the 1990s and has continued sinking roots in workplaces and communities.

The respect we have built up in the 1990s has put us in a good position to intervene with Marxist ideas in the massive struggles that will develop in the next decade. In doing so we will aim to convince as many people as possible, as quickly as possible, of socialist and Marxist ideas and of the need to join our party. However, this is not our only role. Nationally and locally, we always attempt to develop demands and tactics that will take any particular movement forward. In the battle against the poll tax we put forward the slogan 'can't pay, won't pay' and campaigned for organised, mass non-payment of the tax. Even though we had relatively small forces, it was our ability to see which demands would strike a chord with millions of working-class people, which strategy could lead to victory, and then to energetically campaign for our programme and strategy, that made the difference between the success or failure of the movement. Without our role there would still have been mass anger against the poll tax, but it is highly unlikely that it would have taken the form of an organised and democratic mass movement, able to effectively paralyse the efforts of the government through the courts, bailiffs and prisons to impose the tax.

It was not only our strategy, it was also our determination which enabled us to play a leading role. Along with hundreds of others, many Militant supporters, including Terry Fields MP, were jailed for refusing to pay the poll tax.

In hundreds of campaigns, from national movements to local community struggles, we attempt to develop a programme that will take the movement forward. At the same time, we always attempt to link the immediate issues to the broader question: the need to change society.

For a new mass workers' party

In the past, despite its right-wing leadership, most workers saw the Labour Party as 'their party'. In general, this is no longer the case. New Labour is seen as just one more establishment party representing the capitalists. Labour Party membership has fallen by around 100,000 as working-class members have flooded out of the party. Support for Labour in its 'heartlands' has sunk to an all-time low. Even Tony Benn, a socialist who still resists the idea of breaking from the Labour Party, has accepted that, "It is a fact that you cannot find anywhere in Britain more powerful advocates of market forces and globalisation than in the party that describes itself as New Labour."

Even in the past the leaders of the Labour Party generally reflected the interests of the capitalists rather than the working class. However, the working-class membership was able to exert pressure on the leadership through the party's structures. That meant that the capitalists never saw Labour governments as wholly reliable servants of big business. Today the situation is very different. It is true that the trade unions are still affiliated to New Labour. But all the democratic structures, which previously allowed trade unionists and rank-and-file members to influence policy,

a new generation is showing its willingness to struggle

have been dismantled.

There is an urgent need for a new party made up of and representing working-class people. As anger at New Labour grows, the desire for an alternative is also increasing. The government is continuing with its privatisation frenzy at the same time as the trade unions give New Labour money – £6 million in 2001 alone. Unsurprisingly, growing numbers of trade unionists are asking 'why are we feeding the hand that bites us?' At trade union conferences, in the face of hysterical opposition from right-wing leaders, delegates have supported motions moved by Socialist Party members recommending a review of the link with New Labour and considering support for candidates who campaign in the interests of trade unionists. This represents the first tentative steps towards setting up a new party to represent workers' interests. We have seen other foretastes of this in several local elections - including strikers who stood against council cuts in Tameside in the North West, the environmental activists in Killamarsh, and the campaigners for a new comprehensive school who won a council seat in Lewisham, London.

On the basis of their experience of struggle fresh layers of the working class - trade unionists, community campaigners and young people - are drawing the conclusion that they need their own political voice. At the moment this is taking place on a partial and localised level. For a new party made up of, and representing, the working class to develop will take much bigger developments. The Socialist Party recognises that a new party will be formed primarily out of workers' experience in major class battles. These events will push working people to move towards the formation of a new party that represents them. This will probably not happen in one big bang. On the contrary, it could be a confused and drawn-out process with a number of false starts before a new party is successfully created.

However, Socialist Party members do not stand aside and simply wait for objective developments. One of the critical tasks for Marxists is to help the most politically aware sections of workers to draw the conclusion that such a party is necessary and to speed up its formation. Therefore, we raise the need for a new party in our leaflets and other material. We support and encourage any steps that groups of workers take towards that aim. This would include, for example, raising the idea that groups of workers or community campaigners should stand as anti-cuts candidates in elections, or calling for trade unions to open up their political funds to support socialist candidates and disaffiliate from New Labour.

At the same time, the Socialist Party has shown the potential for socialist ideas to gain an echo. We have had important successes in elections, winning four councillors and receiving very good votes in other seats. One of the most effective ways of working towards a new mass workers' party is to support and strengthen the Socialist Party and enable us to reach more workers with our socialist programme.

As well as building the Socialist Party, we also work in broader political

a glimpse at what is possible - one of thousands of new council homes built by the marxist-led liverpool council united alongside the working-class people of the city

formations. This is a vital part of developing any movement. Every struggle we have played a leading role in, including Liverpool City Council and the anti- poll tax campaign, has involved us working as part of broad, democratic left alliances. This holds true in the trade unions where we participate in broad left organisations.

To gain support for socialist ideas and to maximise the socialist vote we are also prepared to take part in 'broad' electoral and general campaigns. It was for this reason that we founded the Socialist Alliance in the mid-1990s. We aimed to bring together different socialist organisations and individuals on a democratic and federal basis. This allowed for the maximum possible principled unity around an agreed set of demands, whilst at the same time preserving the rights of all the separate component parts of the Alliance. Unfortunately, the Socialist Alliance no longer operates on the democratic, federal basis on which it was formed. The very small forces of the Socialist Alliance are now effectively centralised under the control of one organisation, the Socialist Workers Party. For this reason we are currently unable to take part in it, although we are doing our utmost to avoid electoral clashes with it and other socialist organisations. However, the failure of the Socialist Alliance does not alter our enthusiasm for any future formations that represent a step towards a new mass party - be they alliances, electoral agreements or (providing they are organised on a democratic and federal basis) broad socialist parties.

This book gives an outline of the ideas of the Socialist Party. On the basis of events we will adapt and develop our ideas. A vital aspect of this is learning from the struggles of young people and workers but, at the same time, also seeking to generalise this in a programmatic form. Nonetheless, we believe that our ideas are the most effective political tools available to guide the struggle for socialism today. We are therefore engaged in a constant drive to convince as many working-class people as we can reach of our ideas. In the future, when a new mass party of the working class is formed we will, of course, campaign, as the Marxist wing of such a party, for it to adopt our programme. However, it is not certain that we will succeed in the first instance. What we are confident of is that many thousands of workers in Britain will be convinced of our programme and will join the Socialist Party in the coming months and years. We appeal to readers of this book to do so.

We also understand that the broader layers of the working class – 'the millions' - will not all accept our programme on the basis of argumentation alone. The mass of people accept new ideas, not because they read about them in books and newspapers, but on the basis of their own experience. Even then, human consciousness tends to be conservative. It usually lags behind objective reality, although it can then catch up in startling leaps forward. On the basis of their experience over time, the majority of those in a new workers' party could be convinced not only of socialist ideas in general, but of our Marxist programme.

At every stage, locally, nationally and internationally, our party fights to defend the existing position of the working class and for every possible step forward. We fight for the smallest local reforms - such as traffic calming measures on local estates, or fighting for the right to a tea break at work - to more significant steps forward for the working class as a whole, such as a new mass workers' party. However, we never limit ourselves to fighting solely for individual reforms. Throughout all the campaigns we participate in we put the case for socialism. We explain that it is only by overthrowing capitalism, by liberating humanity from the dictates of the market, that we will be able to begin to build a society free from poverty and inequality. That would be a democratic socialist society, driven not by the need to create profits for a few, but the desire to satisfy the needs of all humanity.

our demands

Jobs and work

- A range of policies to achieve full employment, including the introduction of a maximum 35-hour week without loss of pay, a massive increase in public spending in healthcare, housing, education, childcare, leisure and community facilities.
- Implementing the trade union demand for a £5 an hour minimum wage as a step towards £7.50 an hour or £300 a week minimum income (based on the European Decency Threshold). No exemptions. For an annual increase in the minimum wage, linked to average earnings.
- For the right to decent benefits, training or a job without compulsion.
- Employment protection rights for all from day one of employment.
- Scrapping the anti-trade union laws. Trade unions to be democratically controlled by their members. Full-time officials should be regularly elected and receive the wage of an average worker.
- Abolish big-business secrets. Open the books. Let the workers know where all the massive profits, tax rebates and subsidies have gone. No transfers of jobs or production without the agreement of the workers.
- All factories and plant threatened with closure to be brought into public ownership and used for socially-useful production, with compensation only on the basis of proven need.

Public services

- No to the fat cats. Renationalise the privatised utilities under democratic working-class control.
- An immediate £50 a week increase in the pension as a step towards a living pension for all pensioners. Annual increases to be linked to average earnings.
- Free, good-quality education from the nursery to university. A living grant for all students. Abolish the fees now!
- Rebuild the National Health Service, free at the point of use and under democratic control.
- Decent housing with affordable rents. End the housing crisis.
- Major investment into a cheap, accessible, integrated public transport system that meets the needs of the people and the environment.

The environment and food

- A socialist plan for energy production, designed to guarantee cheap and safe energy for all whilst protecting the environment. Such a plan should be worked out by representatives from workers in the energy sector, scientists, community and environmental organisations. The aim would be to replace fossil fuels and nuclear power with massive investment into renewable energy – such as wind, solar and geothermal (extracting heat from the earth's interior) – sources.
- Agribusiness, including the pharmaceutical companies, to be taken into public ownership. For a food processing and retail industry under workers' control to ensure that standards are set by consumers, farm workers and small farmers.

Rights

- The scrapping of the Asylum and Immigration Act and all other racist laws.
- Defend abortion rights. For a woman's right to choose when and whether to have children.
- An end to police harassment. For the abolition of the Criminal Justice Act. Scrap Jack Straw's so-called 'Terrorism' Act. No curtailment of jury trials.
- An end to discrimination on the grounds of race, sex, sexuality, disability and all forms of prejudice.

International and the military

- Abolish third world debt. For the neo-colonial countries to refuse to pay.
- Abolish the IMF and the World Bank.
- Scrap all nuclear weapons. For an immediate and drastic cut in military spending worldwide. A global campaign against chemical and biological weapons.
- Total opposition to Nato. No to a European army.

Fight for socialist change

- For a socialist confederation of England, Scotland, Wales and Ireland.
- For solidarity of the European working class. Oppose the bosses' European Union. No to the euro. For a socialist Europe.
- Take into public ownership the top 150 companies, banks and building societies that dominate the economy, under democratic working-class control and management. Compensation to be paid on the basis of proven need.
- Campaign to form a new mass party of the working class.
- An end to the rule of profit. For a socialist plan of production. For a socialist society and economy run to meet the needs of all whilst protecting our environment.

notes

Britain at the start of the 21st century

1   1998 speech to the CBI annual conference
2   Financial Times, 1 September 2000
3   Captive State - The Corporate Takeover of Britain, George Monbiot
4   ibid

Could things be different?

5   Shelter - Housing and Homelessness in England: The Facts
6   Ibid
7   Britain's Housing in 2022, Joseph Rowntree Foundation
8   Government Housing Statistics Division

Marx was right

9   C H Feinstein, Structural Change in the Developed Countries in the 20th Century, Oxford Review of Economics, 2000
10   IMF report on the US economy, June 1999
11   Wage, Labour and Capital, Karl Marx
12   Dark Heart: the Shocking Truth About Hidden Britain, Nick Davies
13   One World Ready or Not, William Greider

Britain - the world's biggest hedge fund

14   The National Wealth, Dominic Hobson
15   The Observer, 29 October 2000
16   The Guardian, 13 September 2000

How could socialism work?

17 State of the World 1999, Worldwatch Institute
18 One World Ready or Not, William Greider
19 The Independent, 6 July 2002
20 One World Ready or Not, William Greider
21 The Revolution Betrayed, Leon Trotsky
22 Financial Times, 11 February 2002
23   From a study by the economists Richard Vedder, Lowell Gallaway, and David C Clingaman. Source: Stupid White Men, Michael Moore
24 Social Focus on Women, Central Statistical Office 1995
25 George Kennan, US strategic planner, 1948. Source: The New Rulers of the World, John Pilger
26 Source: Ibid

Is there an easier way to change the world?

27 Stupid White Men, Michael Moore
28 All Change at Work? British Employment Relations 1980–1988, Neil Millward, Alex Bryson and John Forth
29 Naomi Klein, The Nation, July 2000
30 The Observer, 13 November 2000
31 The Observer, 13 November 2000
32 Leon Trotsky, The History of the Russian Revolution
33 Leon Trotsky, The Revolution Betrayed
34 Leopold Trepper, The Great Game

bibliography

Jose Bové and François Dutoir, The World is Not for Sale, Verso 2001

Brown, Renner and Halweil, Vital Signs 2000–2001, Earthscan 2000

Nick Davies, Dark Heart, the Shocking Truth about Hidden Britain, Vintage 1998

Clare Doyle, France 1968 – Month of Revolution, Fortress Books 1988

Friedrich Engels, Socialism Utopian and Scientific, Foreign Languages Press, Peking 1975

John Gray, False Dawn: The Delusions of Global Capitalism, Granta 1999

William Greider, One World Ready or Not, Penguin 1998

Dominic Hobson, The National Wealth - Who Gets What in Britain, HarperCollins 1999

Howard, Garnham, Fimister and Veit-Wilson, Poverty – the Facts, Child Poverty Action Group 2001

Naomi Klein, No Logo, Flamingo 2001

Karl Marx/Friedrich Engels, The Communist Manifesto, Various

Karl Marx, Wage, Labour and Capital, Foreign Languages Press, Peking 1975

Karl Marx, Wages, Price and Profit, Foreign Languages Press, Peking 1975

I Meszaros, Marx's Theory of Alienation, Merlin 1986

Millward, Bryson and Forth, All Change at Work? Routledge 2000

George Monbiot, Captive State - The Corporate Takeover of Britain, MacMillan 2000

Michael Moore, Stupid White Men, HarperCollins 2001

John Pilger, The New Rulers of the World, Verso 2002

John Reed, Ten Days that Shook the World, New World Paperbacks 1975

Victor Serge, Year One of the Russian Revolution, Pluto Press 1992

Peter Taaffe, The Rise of Militant, Fortress Books 1995

Peter Taaffe and Tony Mulhearn, Liverpool - a City that Dared to Fight, Fortress Books 1993

Leopold Trepper, The Great Game, Sphere 1979

Leon Trotsky, Marxism in Our Time, old photocopy!

Leon Trotsky, The History of the Russian Revolution, Victor Gollancz Ltd 1965

Leon Trotsky, The Revolution Betrayed, Pathfinder 1987

Francis Wheen, Karl Marx, Fourth Estate 1999

Socialist party

join us	I would like to find out more about / join the Socialist Party ❏
	Name
	Address
	Postcode
	Tel No Email
	Trade Union (if applicable) SOC2102

If you are interested in finding out more about the Socialist Party
or our publications simply fill in this form and return to:
Socialist Party, PO Box 24697, London E11 1YD
email: join@socialistparty.org.uk
tel: 020 8988 8767
website: www.socialistparty.org.uk

Contacting the CWI

The Socialist Party is the English/Welsh section of the Committee for a Workers' International which has affiliated parties and organisations in more than 35 countries on all continents. The way to contact our comrades differs from country to country. Some you can contact directly. For others, it is easier to do it via the CWI offices in London... e-mail to the International Office of the CWI: inter@dircon.co.uk or contact us at PO Box 3688, London, E11 1YE, UK. Telephone: + 44 (0)20 8558 5814. Fax: + 44 (0)20 8988 8793. Our website is on: www.socialistworld.net

If you want to know more about us in... Cyprus, Finland, Kashmir, Pakistan or anywhere else...then contact the CWI international offices above.

Australia: Socialist Party.
PO Box 1015, Collingwood, Victoria 3066.
phone: + 61 3 9650 0160;
e-mail: sp@mira.net
Austria: Sozialistische Linkspartie.
Kaiserstrasse 14/11, 1070 Wien.
phone: + 43 1 524 6310;
fax: + 43 1 524 6311; e-mail: slp@slp.at
Belgium: LSP/MA. PO Box10, 1190 Vorst 3;
phone: + 322 3456181;
e-mail: lspmas@skynet.be
Brazil: Socialismo Revolucionario. Caixa Postal 02009, CEP 01060-970, Sao Paulo S.P. phone: + 55 11 339 5684
e-mail: sr-cio@uol.com.br
Britain: Socialist Party. PO Box 24697, London, E11 1YD. phone: + 44 (0)20 8988 8777; fax: + 44 (0)20 8988 8787;
e-mail: campaigns@socialistparty.org
Canada: Socialist Alternative. 903-633 Bay Street, Toronto, Ontario, MSG 2G4
e-mail: socialistalternative@canada.com
Chile: Celso C Campos, Casilla 50310, Correo Central, Santiago.
phone: + 56 2 622 9004;
e-mail: jandresverra@hotmail.com
CIS: 125167 Moscow a\Ya 37, Moscow.
e-mail: pabgem@online.ru
Czech Republic: Socialistická Alternativa - Budoucnost.
D.V.S., PO Box 227, Bubenské nábřeźi 306, 170 05 Praha 7-Holeŝovice
e-mail: budoucnost@email.cz
France: Les amis de L'Egalite.
Centre 166, 82 rue Jeanne d'Arc, 76000 Rouen. e-mail: grcontact@hotmail.org
Germany: Sozialistische Alternative.
Litten Straße. 106/107, 10179 Berlin.
phone: + 49 302 47 23 802;
e-mail: bundsleitung@sav-online.de
Greece: Xekinima.
8 Gortynos Street, PO Box 11254 Athens.
phone/fax: + 30 1 524 7177;
e-mail: xekinima@hotmail.com
India: Dudiyora Horaata.
PO Box 1828, Bangalore 560018.
e-mail: dudiyorahoraata@usnl.net

Ireland North: Socialist Party.
2nd Floor, 36 Victoria Square, Belfast BT1.
phone: + 44 (0)2890 232962;
fax: + 44 (0)2890 311778;
e-mail: socialist@belfastsp.freeserve.co.uk
Ireland South: Socialist Party.
PO Box 3434, Dublin 8.
phone/fax: + 353 1 677 25 92;
e-mail: info@socialistparty.net
Israel/Palestine: Maavak Sozialisti.
e-mail: info@maavak.org.il
Japan: CWI Japan. Urbain Higashi Mikuni 9-406, Higashi-Mikuni 2-10, Yadokawa–ku, Osaka-shi. phone/fax: + 81 6 396 6998;
e-mail: nixsc@dion.ne.jp
Netherlands: Offensief.
PO Box 11561, 1001 GN Amsterdam.
e-mail: info@offensief.nl
New Zealand:
e-mail: socialist_alternative@hotmail.com
Nigeria: Democratic Socialist Movement.
PO Box 2225, Agege, Lagos.
tel: +234 1492 5671
e-mail: dsm@beta.linkserve.com
Portugal: Alternativa Socialista.
Apartado 27018, 1201-950, Lisboa
e-mail: Alternativa_socialista@clix.pt
Scotland: CWI. PO Box 6773, Dundee, DD1 1YL. phone: + 44 141 221 7714;
South Africa: Democratic Socialist Movement. PO Box 596, Newton, 2113, Johannesburg. phone: + 27 11 342 2220;
e-mail: democraticsocialist@mweb.co.za
Spain: Manifiesto.
Apd. de correos 4435, CP41001, Sevilla
email: meurig@altavista.net
Sri Lanka: United Socialist Party.
261/1 Kirula Road, Narahempito, Colombo 5. phone: + 94 1 508 821
e-mail: usp@wow.lk
Sweden: Rattvisepartiet Socialisterna.
PO Box 73; 123 03 Farsta. phone: + 46 8 605 9400. fax: + 46 8 556 252 52;
e-mail: rs@socialisterna.org
USA: Socialist Alternative.
PO Box 45343, Seatlle, W4, 98145.
e-mail: info@socialistalternative.org